Next Level Cybersecurity

Detect the Signals, Stop the Hack

Sai Huda

Leaders Press

Leaders
Press

ISBN 978-1-943386-41-3 (pbk)

ISBN 978-1-943386-42-0 (ebook)

Library of Congress Control Number: 2019932451

To Gia and Sage, forever blessed

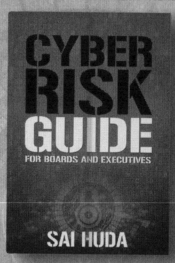

Contents

Chapter 1

The Opening

Chapter 1

The Opening

What do the following have in common?

- ❏ **Facebook** in the United States.
- ❏ **SingHealth** in Singapore.
- ❏ **British Airways** in the United Kingdom.

While they are very different (one is a social-media company, another a healthcare organization and the other an airline), they all had cybersecurity.

And yet the hackers (we'll call them cyber attackers in this book) broke in, evaded the defense, and walked away with valuable data.

Facebook
Cyber attackers got access to the data of 30 million users. They stole details of name, email, phone number and other contact information on 15 million users. They also stole an additional 14 million users' contact information plus profile details, such as username, gender, birth date, device type used to access Facebook, and people or pages the user was following.[1]

SingHealth
Cyber attackers stole the personal information of 1.5 million patients and details of medical prescriptions of 160,000 patients, including the country's prime minister.[2]

British Airways
Cyber attackers stole personal and financial information, such as name, billing address, email, and bank-account and credit-card details, on 380,000 passengers booking flights over a 15-day period.[3]

These three are just a sample of the thousands of organizations worldwide that have fallen victim to cyber attackers stealing or hijacking data or causing other harm. Almost every day, a new victim becomes the headline somewhere in the world.

Every organization — no matter who they are, how large they are, or where they are located in the world — is at risk from cyber attackers.

More than $100 billion each year is spent on information security worldwide and the spending is increasing. Cyber attackers are, however, evading the defense, breaking in, remaining undetected for months, and finding the **Crown Jewels** (these are so important I will highlight them in bold throughout this book). The **Crown Jewels** are essential data, intellectual property and other critical assets.

Cyber attackers are stealing or hijacking the **Crown Jewels** to disrupt operations, causing enormous financial and reputational damage.

They are increasingly operating on behalf of a nation, a rogue state or a criminal organization with deep knowledge and resources.

The attack surface is getting larger for the attackers to exploit:

- ❑ IoT (Internet of Things) devices will grow to an installed base of 25 billion by the end of 2021;[4]
- ❑ Internet users will grow to 6 billion by 2022 (75 percent of the projected world population of 8 billion).[5]

It is only a matter of time before the cyber attackers will break into the network, regardless of whether it is on the premises or in the cloud, and regardless of whether it is outsourced to a supplier. No amount of spending will prevent the cyber attackers from breaking in. There are too many doors, windows and entry points. It is not a question of **IF** but **WHEN**.

So what is an organization to do?

To answer this question, I wrote this book. I researched dozens and dozens of cases worldwide to hunt for the answer to these questions:

- ❑ **Are there patterns of behavior and commonality of steps in the cyber attacks?**
- ❑ **As cyber attackers hunt for the Crown Jewels, are there signals that could detect the attackers in time?**

❑ **What should organizations do differently going forward to avoid becoming the next victim?**

The definition of insanity is to keep doing the same thing while expecting different results. My research revealed that just continuing to spend more money on tools to prevent the cyber attackers from breaking in is not the solution.

Instead the answer is to detect signals of the cyber attackers early, before they are able to steal the **Crown Jewels** or inflict other harm.

Implementing what I describe in this book will transform the defense into offense. By offense, I do not mean striking the cyber attackers, which would have unintended consequences. By offense, I mean proactively detecting the cyber attackers early, before any damage is done, and shutting the threat down.

While organizations are spending money to detect cyber attackers, they are not yet using the method that I describe in this book.

The early-detection method that I have discovered from my research is *the game changer*.

I've spent more than 20 years with companies leading the way in risk and cybersecurity technology to help organizations globally stay one step ahead of the cyber attackers. I've moved them toward a deep understanding of the cybersecurity challenges faced.

Recently, for seven years, as general manager, I led the Risk, Information Security and Compliance business at Fidelity National Information Services, Inc. (FIS), a Fortune 500 company serving more than 20,000 clients globally. Under my leadership, FIS attained the number 1 ranking in Chartis RiskTech100®.

Prior to FIS, I was the founder and CEO of Compliance Coach, Inc., an innovative company providing risk management software and consulting services to more than 1,500 clients in financial services, healthcare and government sectors. We helped clients manage Information Security, Operational and Compliance risks. Compliance Coach was acquired by FIS.

The experience of leading a team of experts to help clients stay ahead of the emerging risks certainly gave me deep insights into the cybersecurity challenges faced by organizations. What hit home, however, was receiving the following notice in the mail, without any warning. (I have redacted some of the information for security and privacy reasons.)

UNITED STATES OFFICE OF PERSONNEL MANAGEMENT
Washington, DC 20415

A	B	C	D	E

PIN NUMBER: ███████████████

Dear SAI HUDA:

As you may know, the Office of Personnel Management (OPM) was the target of a malicious cyber intrusion carried out against the U.S. Government, which resulted in the theft of background investigation records.

You are receiving this notification because we have determined that your ████████████ ████████ was included in the intrusion. As someone whose information was also taken, I share your concern and frustration and want you to know we are working hard to help those impacted by this incident. The Federal government will provide you and your dependent minor children with comprehensive identity theft protection and monitoring services, at no cost to you.

Since you applied for a position or submitted a background investigation form, the information in our records may include your name, Social Security number, address, date and place of birth, residency, educational, and employment history, personal foreign travel history, information about immediate family as well as business and personal acquaintances, and other information used to conduct and adjudicate your background investigation.

Our records also indicate your fingerprints were likely compromised during the cyber intrusion. Federal experts believe the ability to misuse fingerprint data is currently limited. However, this could change over time as technology evolves. Therefore, we are working with law enforcement and national security experts to review the potential ways fingerprint data could be misused now and in the future, and will seek to prevent such misuse. If new means are identified to misuse fingerprint data, additional information and guidance will be made available.

While we are not aware of any misuse of your information, we are providing a comprehensive suite of identity theft protection and monitoring services. We are offering you, and any of your dependent children who were under the age of 18 ████████████ credit monitoring, identity monitoring, identity theft insurance and identity restoration services for ████████ through ████████ a company that specializes in identity theft protection. The identity theft insurance and identity restoration service coverage has already begun. You have access to these services at any time ████████████████ if your identity is compromised.

To take advantage of the additional credit and identity monitoring services, you must enroll with ██ ████ using the PIN code at the top of this letter. To enroll go to ████████████████████ You may also call ████████ to enroll in or ask questions about these services. I hope you will take advantage of these services.

Please note that OPM and ████████ will not contact you to confirm any personal information. If you are contacted by anyone asking for your personal information in relation to this incident, do not provide it. For additional resources such as information you may share with people listed on your forms, sample background investigation forms, types of information which may have been taken, and tips on how to protect your personal information, visit ████████████

Sincerely,

████████████████████

Office of Personnel Management

One of my clients was a large U.S. government agency. My team provided technology and consulting solutions to the client to help manage risks. Given the large size and sensitive nature of the contract, I personally oversaw the relationship. This client required that any supplier doing business with the agency obtain security clearance, which included a comprehensive background check, including fingerprints and family background checks. As the executive overseeing the relationship, I had to obtain security clearance, which I did.

As you can tell from that notice I got in the mail from the U.S. Office of Personnel Management (OPM), which handled background checks for the government agency client, I was one of the 21.5 million people whose information was stolen from OPM in one of the largest data breaches in the government sector globally.

The OPM data breach was not just theft of name, address, email or credit-card information or even social security number. It was much more. It was detailed background information, including driver's license, passport, birth certificate, marriage certificate, credit report, financial information, details of all family, every place lived, neighbors, every place worked, every placed travelled to, even fingerprints.

Along with all of the other victims of this breach, I had been counting on OPM to keep all of my data safe and to detect any cyber attackers trying to get to the data, shut them down and prevent any loss. But this did not happen.

It became clear to me that no organization was immune to a cyber attack and that every organization had to do a better job to protect consumers' information and privacy, because the consumer was counting on it.

From that point on, helping organizations improve cybersecurity to better protect consumers' information and privacy and thwart the cyber attackers became an even stronger passion for me.

In this book, I set out to

❑ explain the **Cyber Attack Chain** — a model that attackers tend to follow in almost every hack;

❑ outline **Cyber Attack Signals** — critical signals of attackers' behavior and activity;

❑ discuss the Top 15 Cyber Attack Signals — 15 signals of attackers in the Cyber Attack Chain that should be the focus;

❑ reveal the Cyber Attack Signals that are typically missed — missed signals in the theft of 3 billion user accounts and in seven other significant cases that provide valuable lessons;

❑ describe in detail a key signal missed — documenting the signal and how in each case it could have detected the attackers in time;

❑ highlight emerging risks with cloud and Internet of Things (IoT) — these are danger zones with a twist where Cyber Attack Signals are critical to detecting the attackers;

❑ show how to perform a **Crown Jewels** analysis and map each **Crown Jewel** to relevant Cyber Attack Signals — a walkthrough of how to implement the early-detection method in seven steps.

In the last chapter of the book, I highlight two emerging risks and backdoors that must be mitigated with the early-detection method. Otherwise, the attackers will exploit them to break in and cause significant damage. These two risks are: supply chain and IoT. I cover the more recent Solar-Winds supply chain hack impacting 18,000 organizations and reveal the Cyber Attack Signals that were missed and how the ASUS hack is a cautionary tale of future IoT attacks and an indicator of another backdoor.

Also, at the end of the book, there is a self-assessment checklist (Appendix A). With it, you can quickly evaluate your cybersecurity and calculate your score out of 100 to assess if you are at risk and identify any gaps or blind spots.

As I cover the seven significant cybersecurity cases in detail, I do not re-hash information you may already know. Instead, I uncover new information that you probably don't know and more importantly the signals that were missed. This allows you to learn from the mistakes of others, so you can improve how you manage cyber risk and stay proactive.

My research involved intensive reviews of each case. I sifted through all of the information to get to the facts and details of each attack. Using that information, I identified what signals were there but were missed.

This book is written so that anyone can quickly and easily read it and gain new learning. It's written to be informative and relevant to you whether you are a student, an employee, a manager, CISO, CIO, CRO, COO, CEO, a board member or just someone curious about why all the headlines keep coming about cyber attacks, data breaches and ransomware even with all of the cybersecurity everywhere.

It does not matter what type of organization you belong to, what sector you are in or what country you are located in. The game changer I describe in this book cuts across all and applies universally.

I have written it in plain language and tried to avoid as much technical jargon as possible, but if I do in some instances, I try to explain it quickly in plain language. I do not insert extraneous information to beef up the chapters and lengthen the book to justify it as a book. I get to the point quickly so that the book will be a quick and enjoyable read. My guiding principle is to reveal something new in each chapter so that you acquire new knowledge and how-to.

I hope you find this book invaluable. Nothing would give me greater joy than to help you take your cybersecurity to the next level so you can detect the cyber attackers early, before any damage is done, shut the threat down, and stay one step ahead.

Chapter 2

The Cyber Attack Chain and Signals

Chapter 2
The Cyber Attack Chain and Signals

Almost every organization, regardless of size, type or industry, faces cyber risk. It could be a small business, mid-size corporation, Fortune 500 company, non-profit, not-for-profit, city or town, state or federal government, located in any country; it does not matter as nearly all face cyber risk.

Why? Because almost every organization has data or other valuable information. This includes a database of customers, members or constituents and information, such as intellectual property, product, sales, financial, payroll, technology or other proprietary information. Its employees, customers, members, constituents and supply chain are using the Internet on a day-to-day basis, and are becoming increasingly reliant on using the Internet to run daily operations. This interconnectivity with and reliance on the Internet creates cyber risk.

Let's take the simple example of email. It is used by almost everyone critical to daily operations and is reliant on the Internet. But cyber attackers can intercept an email while it travels the Internet or can create a fake email and insert a link to a website with malicious code or attach a document with malicious code and send to several employees in an organization. Eventually, the attackers can fool an employee to open the email, activate the malicious code, and unknowingly provide remote access through the Internet to the network. And now the attackers can steal or hijack the data or cause other harm.

This type of reliance on the Internet and the interconnectivity brings cyber risk to almost every organization no matter who they are or where they are located in the world.

Cyber Risk is the risk that an organization — regardless of size, type or industry — faces of adverse impact to operations, earnings, capital or

reputation from cyber attackers stealing data or intellectual property (IP) or committing other compromise, harm or disruption.

Cyber attackers range from individuals to criminal organizations to nations or rogue states. Their objective is to exploit the vulnerabilities in an organization and steal data or IP or commit other compromise, harm or disruption for financial gain or other gain such as competitive, strategic, political or military. No organization is immune to a cyber attack. An organization can suffer enormous harm from the impact of a data breach, theft of IP, other compromise or disruption of operations.

A recent large cyber attack exemplifies the magnitude of the threat faced globally. In this case, the victims were critical industrial organizations in the U.S. targeted by the Russian state. It illustrates how nations have become active aggressive threat actors, beyond criminal gangs or individual hackers, and that all types of organizations across the globe are potential targets of an adversary.

A U.S. Department of Homeland Security (DHS) and Federal Bureau of Investigation (FBI) joint technical alert TA18-074A was titled with the headline "Russian Government cyber activity targeting energy and other critical infrastructure sectors". The alert documented that the following had transpired.[1]

❑ Russian government cyber attackers had targeted organizations in the energy, nuclear, commercial facilities, water, aviation and critical manufacturing sectors in the U.S. The initial victims were trusted third-party suppliers with less secure networks (staging targets). This provided the cyber attackers with the initial entry point and then the capability to penetrate the intended targets.

❑ The cyber attackers used spear phishing emails (targeted emails) to lure the victims to watering holes (websites with compromised web pages masquerading as legitimate to lure the victims either to input their credentials or download malware that enabled theft of user credentials). Once inside the network, the cyber attackers performed internal reconnaissance and moved laterally to hunt for workstations and servers containing information pertaining to Industrial Control Systems (ICS).

❏ The cyber attackers were successful and exfiltrated critical ICS information by copying and then transmitting the copies.

Here is an example of the type of highly sensitive information the cyber attackers exfiltrated. The DHS was able to reconstruct forensically what the attackers stole.

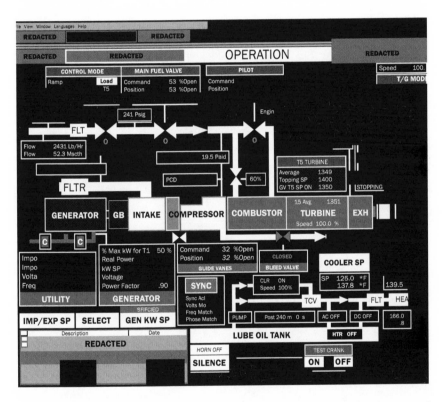

This detailed diagram shows key components of an industrial system, such as generators, compressor, combustor, turbine, cooler, lube oil tank and other items and their dependencies and connectivity. This information could be used to copy and build a similar industrial system or to know where to attack and cause significant havoc and harm.

This was one of the most significant state-sponsored cyber attacks to steal critical strategic infrastructure information, illustrating the magnitude of the threat faced.

Here is a sampling of some of the other larger cyber attacks over the last few years, illustrating the extent and magnitude of the threat faced globally by almost every type of organization. (This list is a sample primarily of data breaches and not distributed denial of service (DDoS) or ransomware attacks that disrupted operations.)

Year	Organization	Sector	Impact
2013	Vodafone	Telecommunications	2 million consumers
2013	Yahoo	Information Services	3 billion user accounts
2013	Adobe	Technology	130 million users
2014	eBay	E-commerce	145 million users
2014	JP Morgan Chase	Financial Services	76 million consumers
2014	Korea Credit Bureau	Financial Services	20 million consumers
2014	Michaels	Retail	3 million consumers
2014	Neiman Marcus	Retail	1.1 million consumers
2014	Home Depot	Retail	56 million consumers
2014	Target	Retail	110 million consumers
2014	Sony	Entertainment	100 million terabytes of records
2015	Anthem	Insurance	78.8 million consumers
2015	U.S. OPM	Government	21.5 million employees, contractors
2015	Hyatt	Hotels	250 locations
2015	Landry's	Restaurants	500 locations
2015	Medical Informatics	Healthcare	3.9 million patients
2015	Premera	Healthcare	11 million patients
2015	Scottrade	Financial Services	4.6 million consumers
2015	UCLA Medical	Healthcare	4.5 million patients
2015	U.K. TalkTalk	Telecommunications	4 million consumers
2016	21st Century Oncology	Healthcare	2.2 million patients
2016	Weebly	E-commerce	43.4 million consumers

2016	U.S. DNC	Politics	50,000 emails and documents
2016	U.S. DHS	Government	30,000 employees
2016	UC Berkeley	Education	80,000 students
2016	Taobao	E-commerce	20 million consumers
2016	Verizon	Telecommunications	1.5 million consumers
2017	South Korea Defense Dept	Military	235 gigabytes of records
2017	Equifax	Financial Services	147.9 million consumers
2017	NHS England	Healthcare	80 hospitals, 6,912 patients
2017	Taringa!	Social Network	28.7 million consumers
2017	Uber	Transportation	57 million individuals
2017	MyHeritage	Genealogy	92.3 million consumers

And more recently

Year	Organization	Sector	Impact
2018	BMO / Simpli	Financial Services	90,000 consumers
2018	UnderArmour	Retail	150 million consumers
2018	SingHealth	Healthcare	1.5 million patients
2018	T-Mobile	Telecommunications	2 million consumers
2018	British Airways	Airlines	380,000 consumers
2018	Facebook	Social Media	30 million accounts
2018	Cathay Pacific	Airlines	9.4 million consumers
2018	Marriott	Hotels	383 million consumers
2019	Capital One	Financial Services	106 million consumers
2019	DoorDash	Food Delivery	4.9 million consumers
2019	First American	Financial Services	885 million files
2019	Quest Diagnostics	Healthcare	11.9 million patients
2019	LifeLabs	Healthcare	15 million patients
2020	Wishbone	Social Network	40 million records
2020	MGM Resorts	Hotels	142 million consumers
2020	Animal Jam	Gaming	46 million records
2020	SolarWinds	Technology	18,000 customers

To illustrate the magnitude of cyber risk further, let's consider the following scenario. It is beyond loss of money, data, IP or other harm.

It is midnight Saturday at a hospital. It is the middle of the summer with a heatwave. There are 100 patients in the air-conditioned Emergency Room (ER) and Intensive Care Unit (ICU) in beds receiving lifesaving critical care.

Suddenly, all of the personal computers and laptops used by doctors and nurses become frozen in ER, in ICU and throughout the hospital. Several items of medical equipment stop functioning. Doctors and nurses are unable to look up medical records and provide required medical care and medicines to the patients. There is complete chaos.

While medical staff and management try to figure out what has happened and try to focus on the patients with the most critical condition, several patients' medical conditions start to deteriorate. After four hours, all of a sudden, the problem goes away and the computers and medical equipment are restored. By this time, five patients in ER and ICU have died and a dozen are in more critical condition.

The CEO of the hospital then receives an email that says unless $1M in cryptocurrency payment is made within the next two hours, the same situation will occur again.

While this loss-of-life scenario has not yet happened, it is not far-fetched and could happen. Later in the book, I walk you through seven significant cases illustrating cyber risk and one of them was a case where cyber attackers came close to causing deaths even though they were after financial gain.

In order to manage cyber risk effectively, we must first understand the Cyber Attack Chain.

The Cyber Attack Chain is a model that depicts the steps that cyber attackers tend to follow in almost every cyber attack. It is a simplified model to enable early focus on the detection of the cyber attackers, because once the cyber attack is executed, it is too late.

❑ Lockheed Martin first developed a model, Intrusion Kill Chain, composed of seven phases.[2]

❏ MITRE developed the Cyber Attack Lifecycle, composed of seven phases and eleven steps.[3]

❏ Mandiant developed the Attack Lifecycle, comprised of eight phases.[4]

Based on a review of these three models and my research into dozens and dozens of cases to identify patterns of behavior and commonality of steps taken by cyber attackers, I have developed this Cyber Attack Chain.

Figure 1. Cyber Attack Chain

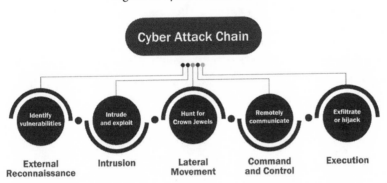

The Cyber Attack Chain has five overall steps that cyber attackers tend to follow in almost every attack.

❖ external reconnaissance

The cyber attackers research and identify the target and its vulnerabilities to exploit.

❖ intrusion

The cyber attackers intrude and start to exploit the vulnerabilities.

❖ lateral movement

The cyber attackers then takes steps to maintain presence and start to move around to hunt for the **Crown Jewels**.

❖ command and control

The cyber attackers firm up command and control communications remotely and prepare for the asset exfiltration or accomplishment of other objective.

❖ execution

The cyber attackers execute the asset exfiltration or other objective.

At each step, the cyber attackers will take great care to avoid detection and will try to hide, but as they perform the tasks at each step there will be signals of the cyber attackers at work.

External reconnaissance (Step 1) is early in the cycle and the signals may not materialize into a cyber attack, while execution (Step 5) is late in the cycle and detecting signals at this stage will probably be too late because the asset exfiltration or other objective would have been accomplished by this time.

It is in the intrusion, lateral movement and command and control (Steps 2-4) where detecting signals of the cyber attackers will be of greatest value, because these steps are as the cyber attackers intrude but before the cyber attack is executed.

It is only a matter of time before the cyber attackers will intrude. It is impossible to prevent intrusion. Once the cyber attack is executed, it is too late, so early detection of the cyber attackers, prior to the execution of the cyber attack is the secret to stopping the hack and avoiding a loss.

My research into the dozens and dozens of cases worldwide revealed that cyber attackers followed the Cyber Attack Chain and that in each step, as they hunted for the **Crown Jewels**, their behaviors and activities provided signals.

In each case, however, these signals were either not monitored or missed by the organization or if someone did notice an anomaly, they either did not recognize it as a signal or it was never followed up. Senior management and board oversight was missing or inadequate, so the attackers slipped through the cybersecurity, and stole the data, or inflicted other harm.

Based on researching these cases, it became evident that as the attackers move through the Cyber Attack Chain, there will be signals, and detecting these signals at Steps 2-4 will be of greatest value because the hack can be stopped in time and any loss avoided.

In the next chapter, I define what a Cyber Attack Signal is and reveal the Top 15 Cyber Attack Signals.

Five key takeaways from this chapter

❑ Every organization worldwide is exposed to **Cyber Risk**. It is the risk of adverse impact to operations, earnings, capital or reputation from cyber attackers stealing data or intellectual property (IP) or committing other compromise, harm or disruption.

❑ The **Cyber Attack Chain** is a simplified model that captures the five overall steps that cyber attackers tend to follow in almost every attack. The five steps are external reconnaissance, intrusion, lateral movement, command and control, and execution.

❑ Research into dozens and dozens of cases worldwide revealed that cyber attackers followed the Cyber Attack Chain and in each step, as they hunted for the **Crown Jewels** (data, intellectual property or other critical assets), their behaviors and activities provided **Cyber Attack Signals**.

❑ Based on researching these cases, it became evident that as the attackers move through the Cyber Attack Chain, detecting these signals in the intrusion, lateral movement and command and control steps (Steps 2-4) will be of greatest value.

❑ It is only a matter of time before the cyber attackers will intrude. It is impossible to prevent intrusion. Once the cyber attack is executed, it is too late, so **early detection** of the cyber attackers prior to the execution of the cyber attack is the secret to stopping the hack and avoiding a loss.

Chapter 3

Early Detection is the Game Changer

Chapter 3

Early Detection is the Game Changer

The Study on Global Megatrends in Cybersecurity, sponsored by Raytheon and independently conducted by Ponemon Institute, provides new insights into the most critical cyber-threat trends emerging over the next three years through the eyes of those on the frontline of cybersecurity.[1]

More than 1,110 senior information-technology practitioners around the world were surveyed.

The study revealed key insights and predictions from the expert practitioners for the next three years, such as:

Cyber extortion and data breaches impacting shareholder value will increase.

- ❏ 67 percent said risk of cyber extortion, such as ransomware, will increase in frequency and payout.
- ❏ 66 percent said their organization will experience a data breach or cybersecurity exploit that will seriously diminish shareholder value.
- ❏ 60 percent predicted state-sponsored attacks will become even worse.
- ❏ Only 41 percent said their organization will be able to minimize Internet of Things (IoT) risks.

The frequency of cyber extortion, nation-state attacks and attacks against industrial controls were predicted to increase by double-digits.

- ❏ 19 percent said cyber extortion is very frequent today, while 42 percent said this threat will be very frequent over the next three years.
- ❏ 26 percent said nation-state attacks are very frequent today, while 45 percent said this will be very frequent over the next three years.

❑ 40 percent said attacks against industrial controls and supervisory control and data acquisition (SCADA) systems are very frequent today, while 54 percent said this will be very frequent over the next three years.

Loss or theft of data from unsecured Internet of Things (IoT) devices is likely to happen and is a significant cybersecurity challenge.

❑ 82 percent said it is very likely, likely or somewhat likely that their organization will have a loss or theft of data caused by an unsecured IoT device or application.
❑ 80 percent said likelihood of a security incident related to an unsecured IoT device or application could be catastrophic.

In summary, Raytheon and Ponemon Institute's Study on Global Megatrends in Cybersecurity provides several predictions from cybersecurity practitioners across the globe, who are on the frontline defending against the cyber attackers daily. Among them, over the next three years, even with all of the increased spending on cybersecurity:

❑ cyber extortion and data breaches will greatly increase in frequency. This trend will largely be driven by sophisticated state-sponsored cyber attackers or organized groups.
❑ IoT devices in particular are very susceptible and will be targets that will be exploited.

So it is not a question of **IF** but **WHEN** the cyber attackers will break in. And when the cyber attackers break in, they will remain undetected for many months.

The median or mean number of days the cyber attackers remain undetected varies based on the source. Examples are:

❑ Mandiant's M-Trends Report;
❑ Verizon's Data Breach Investigations Report;
❑ IBM and Ponemon Institute's Cost of a Data Breach Study.

One thing is certain, however. The cyber attackers are able to hide for many months and the longer it takes to detect the cyber attackers, the more the cost the organization ends up suffering.

Based on a research into dozens and dozens of cases, I have identified signals in the Cyber Attack Chain that every organization should understand and look for.

When researching the cases, it became evident that in each case, the cyber attackers took steps that fit into one of the steps as I have outlined in the Cyber Attack Chain. It was also clear that in each step, there were signals of the cyber attackers at work, but that these signals were not detected by the organization.

It is time for every organization to understand what the Cyber Attack Signals are, and implement them as part of their cybersecurity program. By doing so, they will transform the defense into offense and detect the cyber attackers early.

A Cyber Attack Signal is a high-probability signal of cyber attackers at work, trying to hide and avoid detection, while performing one of the tasks in the Cyber Attack Chain. They are at work to accomplish their ultimate objective — the theft of data or intellectual property (IP) or other compromise, harm or disruption. A Cyber Attack Signal focuses on cyber attackers' behavior.

I have identified 15 Cyber Attack Signals that, as a minimum, every organization should focus its monitoring on. These Top 15 signals relate to cyber attackers' behavior. They are timely signals, before the cyber attack is executed, occurring at the intrusion, lateral movement or command and control steps of the Cyber Attack Chain, and are, therefore, of greatest value.

This is not an exhaustive list and there will probably be other signals relevant to an organization based on its risk profile and its **Crown Jewels** that may indicate the cyber attackers at work. As such, each organization should tailor its list of Cyber Attack Signals for monitoring.

Intrusion

❑ **patch window**
This is the time period a vulnerability remains unpatched and also how attackers could exploit it, providing an alert about **Crown Jewels** possibly impacted, probable attack timeline and expected attacker behavior.

❑ **web shell**
This is the attempted installation or installation of a web shell to a web server. It would exploit server or application vulnerabilities or configuration weaknesses to make the intrusion.

Lateral movement

❑ **abnormal logons**
These are anomalies in logons compared to normal logon patterns.

❑ **privileged users' behavior**
These are anomalies in the behavior of privileged users (users with greater access levels and capabilities) compared to normal behavior.

❑ **WMI anomalies**
This is abnormal activity with Windows Management Instrumentation (WMI), a set of tools for system administrators to manage Windows systems locally and remotely.

❑ **internal reconnaissance signals**
These are anomalies in scripts or batch scripts running on email, web and file servers or domain controller or hosts, or scanning of servers and ports.

❑ **malware signals**
These are anomalies from normal behavior patterns in terms of users, files, processes, tasks, sources and destination to indicate initial malware installation or propagation.

❑ **ransomware signals**

This is anomalous activity to indicate initial ransomware installation or propagation, such as installation of new .dll file or attempted communication with a TOR website (i.e. server on the TOR network, a service used to provide anonymity over the Internet.)

❑ **malicious PowerShell**

This is abnormal activity with PowerShell, a scripting language for system administrators to automate tasks, such as odd characters (e.g. + ' $ %) added in the scripts, use of "powershell.exe" by abnormal users at unusual times or locations or scripts containing command parameters.

❑ **RDP signals**

These are anomalies with Remote Desktop Protocol (RDP), which enables a user (e.g. as help-desk staff) to use a graphical interface to connect to another computer in a network, such as abnormal RDP users, source or destination logons.

❑ **SMB anomalies**

These are anomalies with Server Message Block (SMB), a protocol in Microsoft Windows that enables remotely managing files, file sharing, printing and directory share among other functions in a network.

❑ **unusual logs behavior**

These are anomalies in event logs, such as event logs removed, stopped or cleared with details (user details, date, time, type of log, command executed, asset impacted, source and destination).

Command and control

❑ **C&C communications**

This is anomalous activity indicating attempted communication or communications with a command and control (C&C) server, such as a request to an unusual domain name or a one-off domain name, a request to numeric IP address as domain name for host, requests to certain IP addresses or hosts with certain frequency (hourly, daily or other).

❑ **ICMP packets**
These are anomalies with Internet Control Message Protocol (ICMP) packets, such as abnormal size, frequency, source or destination.

❑ **hidden tunnels**
These are anomalies of HTTP, HTTPS or DNS traffic compared to normal baseline patterns indicating communications with a C&C server using a tunnel designed to blend in with normal traffic.

Appendix B provides further details on each of the Top 15 Cyber Attack Signals.

While I explain later in the book what should be considered **Crown Jewels** and show how to map to applicable Cyber Attack Signals, this list of 15 is a solid foundation and a good starting point for the organization to consider as it determines which signals it should focus its monitoring on and transform the defense into offense.

An organization should develop a dashboard of Cyber Attack Signals to focus its monitoring and for reporting to the highest levels. Either its own security information and event management (SIEM) system or its cloud-hosting provider, such as Amazon Web Services (AWS), Microsoft Azure or Google Cloud, will produce many signals. The organization will, however, in order to be effective, need to determine the list of critical Cyber Attack Signals to focus the monitoring on and to report to the highest levels of the organization, based on the **Crown Jewels** and its risk profile.

Ultimately, it is the organization that owns cybersecurity, regardless of whether it has outsourced the network to a cloud infrastructure and services provider (such as AWS, Microsoft or Google).

The organization is responsible for security *in* the cloud, whereas the cloud provider is responsible for security *of* the cloud.

Whether on the premises or in the cloud, the key to success is to make sure the Cyber Attack Signals focus on detecting cyber attackers' behavior early. I explain more on this later in the book.

Implementing Cyber Attack Signals is *the game changer*.

Why? Because it enables an organization to cut through all of the noise and focus on the **Crown Jewels** and the signals that will most probably detect the cyber attackers early and significantly increases the chance to prevent the cyber attackers from accomplishing their objective.

Here are the Top 15 Cyber Attack Signals depicted visually in the Cyber Attack Chain in the intrusion, lateral movement and command and control steps.

Figure 1. Top 15 Cyber Attack Signals in the Cyber Attack Chain

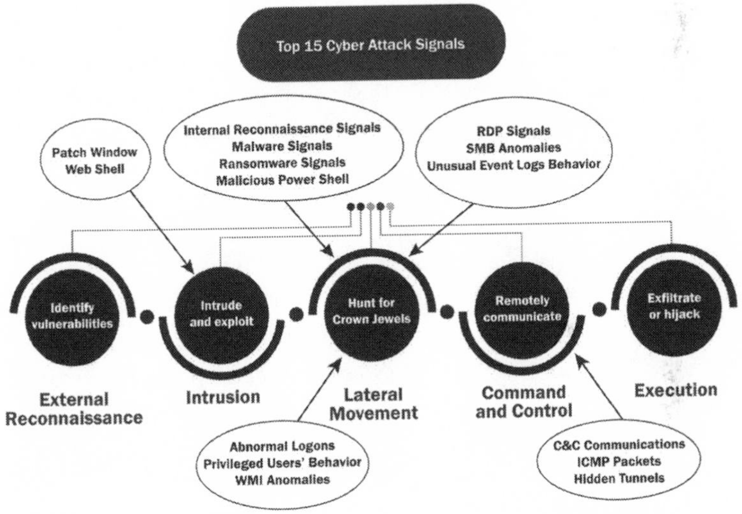

While, in Figure 1, the Cyber Attack Chain shows each Cyber Attack Signal in a particular step, this is based on generally when the signal is more likely to detect the cyber attackers.

It is possible, however, the Cyber Attack Signal may detect the cyber attackers in a different step, depending on the particulars of the cyber attack.

For example, while the Cyber Attack Chain shows malware signals will most probably detect the attackers installing malware in the lateral movement step, it is possible the cyber attackers may intrude using a malware and the malware signals could also detect this earlier in the intrusion step.

Another example is that while the Cyber Attack Chain shows C&C communications will most probably detect the attackers communicating with its C&C server in the command and control step, it is possible the cyber attackers may intrude using a malware and immediately call back to a C&C server to confirm success of the malware installation, and the C&C communications could also detect this earlier in the intrusion step.

The Cyber Attack Signals depicted in the Cyber Attack Chain, therefore, reflect generally when the signal is more likely to detect the cyber attackers, but the signal may also detect the cyber attackers in a different step, depending on the particulars of the cyber attack.

The Top 15 Cyber Attack Signals represent multiple signals that provide multiple opportunities to detect the cyber attackers early. If one signal is missed for some reason at a step, another signal can detect the attackers at another step, before damage is done.

MITRE's Cyber Analytics Repository (CAR) provides a suite of cyber attack behavioral detection analytics.[2] This is another valuable resource to consult when developing the Cyber Attack Signals appropriate for the organization.

According to MITRE's technical report *Finding Cyber Threat with AT-T&CK-Based Analytics*, cyber attackers exhibit consistent patterns of behavior post-intrusion. Results of MITRE's research indicated that focusing on signals of cyber attackers' behavior post-intrusion using analytics provides a practical way to separate all of the noise generated from normal system use to detect the cyber attackers.

MITRE validated its research findings on both the behavioral analytics and the efficacy of using the analytics to detect the cyber attackers through a series of cyber games using a Red Team (i.e. team emulating the cyber attackers) against a Blue Team (i.e. team using the analytics to detect the Red Team) on a 250-node production enclave on MITRE's live corporate network.[3]

Another valuable source to consult when developing the Cyber Attack Signals is Open Web Application Security Project (OWASP)'s resources, such as the OWASP Top 10,[4] which lists the most impactful application security risks facing organizations and the OWASP Top Internet of Things (IoT) Vulnerabilities, which lists the vulnerabilities and associated attack surfaces.[5]

Cyber attackers are increasingly hunting for vulnerabilities in applications and IoT devices because they have realized that these constitute another gateway and frequently provide a quicker path to the **Crown Jewels** due to wide range of exposures in both.

For example with IoT, frequently the IoT devices are built by manufacturers and shipped without prioritizing security and thinking through on how attackers could exploit the devices. For example with software development, delays in implementing patches to known vulnerabilities, errors in code reviews that miss detecting components with known vulnerabilities, failing to monitor logs relating to software development activities, or using cloud-based tools for accelerated software development while letting the guard down on normal security precautions. These exposures create additional paths for cyber attackers to exploit.

The OWASP Top 10 is based on an industry survey of more than 500 security professionals covering vulnerabilities spanning more than 100,000 applications and application programming interfaces (APIs). The Top 10 list of application security risks is selected and prioritized based on feedback from the survey respondents on exploitation, detection and impact assessments. The Top IoT Vulnerabilities lists the top vulnerabilities that cyber attackers can exploit in IoT devices and the associated attack surfaces.

The list of the Top 15 Cyber Attack Signals is based on reviewing MITRE and OWASP resources as well as researching dozens and dozens of cases. These signals focus on detecting cyber attackers' behavior in the steps of the Cyber Attack Chain where there is greatest value (i.e. intrusion, lateral movement and command and control).

In the next few chapters, I walk you through the Cyber Attack Signals in more detail, while covering seven significant cybersecurity cases. In each of these cases, there were multiple signals, but they were not detected. Had the organizations detected the signals, the cyber attackers would most probably have been foiled.

In each case, I point out the various signals missed, but also explain in detail a key Cyber Attack Signal missed in the Cyber Attack Chain and how the organization could have detected the attackers in time. Each of these cases is a great learning opportunity.

We're going to dig into the following significant cases that happened over the last few years and reveal the new, deep-dive discoveries:

Organization	Sector	Key Signal Missed	Impact
Equifax	Financial Services	patch window	179.9 million consumers
Anthem	Insurance	abnormal logons	78.8 million consumers
U.S. OPM	Government	privileged users' behavior	21.5 million employees
NHS England	Healthcare	ransomware signals	80 hospitals, 6,912 patients
U.S. DNC	Politics	unusual logs behavior	50,000 documents
Target	Retail	ICMP packets	110 million consumers
SingHealth	Healthcare	C&C communications	1.5 million patients

Also, in the last chapter of the book, we will cover the more recent Solar-Winds hack. This is one of the largest hacks in history, highlighting supply chain risk. The hack of SolarWinds, a cybersecurity software provider to 300,000 organizations worldwide, impacted 18,000 of its customers. We will reveal the key Cyber Attack Signals missed and how the hack could have been detected in time.

Five key takeaways from this chapter

❏ A **Cyber Attack Signal** is a high-probability signal of the cyber attackers at work while performing one of the tasks in the Cyber Attack Chain. They are at work to accomplish their ultimate objective — the theft of data or intellectual property (IP) or other compromise, harm or disruption. A Cyber Attack Signal focuses on cyber attackers' behavior.

❏ Implementing Cyber Attack Signals is the game changer. It enables an organization to cut through all of the noise and focus on the **Crown Jewels** and the **Cyber Attack Signals** that will most probably detect the cyber attackers early and significantly increases the chance to prevent the cyber attackers from accomplishing their objective.

❏ Based on research into dozens and dozens of cases, it became evident that in each case, the cyber attackers took steps that fit into one of the steps outlined in the Cyber Attack Chain, but also in each step there were signals of the cyber attackers at work, but these signals were not detected by the organization.

❏ The **Top 15 Cyber Attack Signals** are based on the signals missed in dozens and dozens of cases and focuses on cyber attackers' behavior and provide timely signals, before the cyber attack is executed (i.e. in intrusion, lateral movement and command and control steps in the Cyber Attack Chain).

❏ While each of the Top 15 Cyber Attack Signals are shown in a particular step of the Cyber Attack Chain, this is based on generally when the signal is more likely to detect the cyber attackers. It is possible, however, that the signal may detect the cyber attackers in a different step, depending on the particulars of the cyber attack. The Top 15 signals represent multiple signals that provide multiple opportunities to detect the attackers early. If one signal is missed for some reason at a step, another signal can detect the attackers at another step, before damage is done.

Chapter 4

Missed Signals in 3 Billion User Accounts Theft

Chapter 4

Missed Signals in 3 Billion User Accounts Theft

Before we dig into the seven cases, we must begin with a recap of the Yahoo case. After all, Yahoo suffered a massive data breach impacting 3 billion user accounts and the case provides several critical opening lessons as we proceed to the other cases.

Yahoo actually suffered several cyber attacks over the years beginning in 2008. But it was the 2013 and 2014 attacks and data breaches that were the most impactful and provide the opening lessons.

Yahoo is now a part of Verizon and its subsidiary, Oath. Verizon completed its acquisition of Yahoo on June 13, 2017.[1] Verizon ended up paying $350 million less than what it originally agreed to buy Yahoo for. About a year earlier, on July 25, 2016, Verizon had announced it would acquire Yahoo for $4.83 billion.[2]

A year later, after learning of Yahoo's data breaches, Verizon purchased Yahoo for $4.48 billion, a discount of $350 million. Yahoo had to agree to assume 50 percent of any liabilities from third-party litigation or from any non-U.S. Securities and Exchange Commission (SEC) government investigations and pay 100 percent of any liabilities from shareholder lawsuits and SEC investigations.[3]

Yahoo, now a part of Verizon's Oath subsidiary, is a multinational technology company that provides a web portal, search engine, email, news, advertising, microblogging and social networking to more than 1 billion monthly active users, including 600 million monthly active mobile users worldwide.

Yahoo derives most of its revenues from advertising through search, display and native advertising, including mobile advertising. It provides targeted advertisements to users based on their personal information. Yahoo collects and stores information on its users, such as users' names, email addresses, telephone numbers, birth dates, passwords and security questions.

Given the scale of its reach and the size of user data stored, it was a target of periodic cyber attacks, beginning in 2008. The user data was of tremendous value to cyber attackers.

Just take by itself the email address of a user that Yahoo had in its user database (UDB). Stealing just the email would be of significant value to a cyber attacker.

A stolen email address can be exploited in many ways.

❑ **Account takeover**
Frequently, the email address is the username in many accounts, ranging from email to social media to bank accounts.

❑ **Phishing**
The email address can be used to perpetrate phishing and use malware to steal other credentials.

❑ **Identity theft**
The email address has become a critical identity attribute and can be used to perpetrate a variety of fraud, ranging from employment fraud to financial fraud.

The email address, along with all of the other personal information of users that Yahoo had in its UDB, was very attractive to cyber attackers all along and Yahoo continued to get attacked from 2008 onwards, but it was the two major data breaches in 2013 and 2014 that led to the $350 million discounted sale price, along with other financial and reputational impact.

In August 2013, cyber attackers broke into Yahoo and stole 3 billion users' account information. Initially, Yahoo reported that it was 1 billion users' accounts that were stolen, but finally, on October 3, 2017, Yahoo disclosed that the 2013 breach involved 3 billion users' accounts.[4]

Even when Yahoo initially said it was 1 billion users who were impacted, analysts were calling it the "Exxon Valdez of security breaches" and in order to highlight the magnitude of the breach, underlined that the theft involved 1 billion accounts and there were only 3 billion people in the world with Internet access at that time.[5]

The cyber attackers broke into the email system of Yahoo and stole names, email, birth dates, phone numbers, hashed passwords (which could easily be cracked since Yahoo was using MD5, an outdated security mechanism), security questions and the backup email addresses to reset the passwords.

The stolen backup email address was of great value to the cyber attackers because frequently it was a user's work email address in case they were ever locked out of their Yahoo account. So users such as government or military employees would be of even greater value to the cyber attackers since they could now tell where they worked and could specifically target those users to hack into their personal or email accounts, posing an increased threat to national security.

The attackers also forged the cookies that Yahoo places on user computers to gain access to the user accounts without ever having the user's password since the forged cookie would allow the attackers to remain logged into a user's account indefinitely.

Yahoo was slow to disclose the August 2013 data breach and finally did so on December 14, 2016.

The 2014 data breach, according to the U.S. Grand Jury Indictment filed on February 28, 2017, was perpetrated by intelligence officers of Russia's Federal Security Service (FSB) and several criminal co-conspirators who were paid by the FSB officers to hack into Yahoo's network.

The indictment lays out in detail how beginning early in 2014, the cyber attackers broke into Yahoo's network and began reconnaissance. Malicious files and software tools were downloaded onto Yahoo's network. Several months later, the cyber attackers located Yahoo's **Crown Jewels** — the UDB and Account Management Tool (AMT).[6]

The UDB contained users' personal information, including username, backup or recovery email address, phone numbers, password challenge questions and answers and certain cryptographic security information associated with the account.

The AMT allowed access to and editing of the information stored in the UDB. It also allowed password changes or making, logging or tracking other changes to user accounts in the UDB.

Then, in November 2014, the cyber attackers used stolen Yahoo employee credentials to log into UDB hosts and the AMT, and they also found where the weekly UDB backup files were stored. The attackers moved the UDB backup files to a compromised server in the network, and then copied portions of the backup files and transmitted out via FTP connection to a host server in Russia. The attackers then deleted the UDB backup file from the compromised server to hide the trail and avoid detection.

More than 500 million users' account information was stolen by the cyber attackers.

Access to the AMT allowed the attackers to access information about particular user accounts. The attackers also used a malicious script placed on Yahoo's network to mint cookies in bulk (up to at least tens of thousands of cookies at a time) to access more than 30 million users' accounts.

The attackers also took steps to avoid detection by installing a program into Yahoo's network known as a log cleaner to delete logs of network activity.

Yahoo again was slow to disclose the data breach and finally disclosed the theft of 500 million users' account information on September 22, 2016.[7]

It was not until March 1, 2017 that it disclosed that there were forged cookies for 32 million users' accounts related to the 2014 data theft.[8]

Multiple federal and state class-action lawsuits were filed against Yahoo. Multiple regulatory investigations commenced in the U.S. and in other countries. The U.S. Securities and Exchange Commission (SEC) began an investigation. On April 24, 2018, the SEC fined Yahoo $35 million to settle charges that it misled investors by failing to disclose the data breaches, but it continues its investigation.[9] The class-action lawsuits inevitably will also result in multi-million dollar settlements.

The Yahoo case provides several opening lessons, as we proceed to dig into the other significant cases.

Five key takeaways from this chapter

❑ Cybersecurity must be a priority for every organization, starting at the highest level (board and senior management). Otherwise, it will be costly both financially and reputationally, and may even be catastrophic. In Yahoo's case, it was almost catastrophic and certainly costly ($350 million discount on the sale price, $35 million SEC penalty, millions spent on post-breach risk mitigation, millions to be spent to settle the class-action lawsuits and more).

❑ Cyber attackers will break in, so the focus must be on early detection. Consider the attacker activities and the signals that were there but were not detected by Yahoo in the Cyber Attack Chain:
- **lateral movement**
  - ✓ internal reconnaissance by the attackers in the network looking for the **Crown Jewels**;
  - ✓ stolen employee credentials used by the attackers to log into UDB and the AMT;
  - ✓ moving the UDB backup copy files to a compromised server inside the network;
  - ✓ deleting the UDB backup copy files;
  - ✓ deleting logs of network activity using the log cleaner.
- **command and control**
  - ✓ periodic communications with attackers command and control server when minting cookies;
  - ✓ downloading malicious files and software tools (e.g. log clearing) into the network from attackers command and control server;

✓ using the internal FTP server to transmit portions of UDB backup copy files to attackers' C&C server in Russia.

❑ Each organization must focus on the **Crown Jewels** and stay one step ahead of the cyber attackers by looking for signals of the attackers trying to get to the **Crown Jewels**. Yahoo did not focus on monitoring signals of cyber attackers on the path to the **Crown Jewels**, the UDB and AMT.

❑ Once cyber attackers are detected, prompt risk-mitigation action must be taken to eliminate the attackers, but also to prevent a repeat of the attackers' intrusion, lateral movement and command and control. Yahoo was slow and did not take prompt risk-mitigation action and the attackers continued to attack and were repeatedly successful at stealing data.

❑ Yahoo **missed** many **Cyber Attack Signals** that could have detected the cyber attackers **early**, and the hack could have most probably been stopped in time before the massive theft of data of 3 billion user accounts.

Chapter 5

Equifax: Patch Window

Chapter 5
Equifax: Patch Window

Most breaches occur because cyber attackers exploit vulnerabilities and break into the network before the vulnerabilities are either patched or before an interim workaround defense is implemented to keep the cyber attackers out, while the patch is being worked on. This is what I call the *patch window*.

The patch window is the time period between a known vulnerability and the fix (i.e. the patch). It is the number of days a vulnerability remains unpatched, but also highlights the vulnerability type and how the attackers could exploit it, providing an alert as to which **Crown Jewels** might be targets given the specific vulnerability, the probable attack timeline and attackers' expected behavior.

Vulnerabilities become known from either self-scanning, code reviews or penetration tests performed by an organization as part of its routine cybersecurity practices or from security alerts made publicly or privately by government bodies or industry groups. Sometimes vulnerabilities are also made known to the organization by outside security researchers.

Patching the vulnerabilities promptly with a sense of urgency is critical, especially with the vulnerabilities that are publicly made known, since the cyber attackers also become aware of it at the same time. It becomes a race against the cyber attackers in the patch window either to patch or to put a workaround defense in place while the patch is being worked on before the cyber attackers get into the network.

The patch window challenge is made even more difficult when the vulnerability is made known publicly from a security alert and the patch is not made available at the same time as the alert. Sometimes the patch may follow the alert a few days later due to the complexity of the vulnerability.

Even if the patch is made available at the same time as the security alert is published publicly, if either the patch or the workaround defense is not immediately implemented, the cyber attackers can take advantage of the patch window and break in.

Frequently, the patch itself cannot be implemented immediately due to the complexity of the vulnerability and the impact to the code, applications and servers. It is not simply a matter of pushing an update button and re-booting, or a copy, paste and replace of the code. Frequently, it involves analyzing existing code to make sure not to break anything in the process or finding developers who are familiar with the existing code or the new code, since the vulnerability may involve code, applications or servers from several years ago, and there needs to be sufficient testing prior to pushing it out to production.

So it may take a while to put the patch in and resolve the vulnerability. That is why if the patch cannot be implemented right away, an interim work-around defense must be implemented immediately upon receiving the security alert. Otherwise the cyber attackers can exploit the vulnerability during the patch window.

Not all vulnerabilities, including those made known publicly, are equal. Some are extremely high risk and critical and must be prioritized and addressed immediately.

MITRE's Common Vulnerabilities and Exposures (CVE) is an industry standardized list of entries, each containing an identification number, a description and at least one public reference, for publicly known cybersecurity vulnerabilities.[1]

CVE entries are posted in MITRE's CVE website and in the U.S. National Vulnerability Database.[2]

CVE is now the industry standard for vulnerability and exposure identifiers. CVE entries are also called CVEs, CVE IDs and CVE numbers. The CVE entries are used in numerous cybersecurity products and services around the world.

The CVEs are categorized into risk levels with Common Vulnerability Scoring System (CVSS) score ranges from 0-1 to 9-10, with 9-10 categorized as a critical level. The CVSS score enables prioritization of vulnerability remediation and identifying the severity of the vulnerability.

Each CVE entry includes

- ❑ a CVE ID number (e.g. CVE-2019-1001);
- ❑ a description of the security vulnerability or exposure;
- ❑ any pertinent references (e.g. vulnerability reports or advisories).

Vulnerabilities with a CVSS score of 8-9 and 9-10 in particular must be prioritized and addressed immediately after discovery or receiving a security alert. If the patch is not available or cannot be immediately implemented, an interim workaround defense must be implemented immediately in the patch window to prevent cyber attackers from breaking in before the fix and causing a cyber disaster.

This is what was not achieved in the case of the Equifax breach, one of the largest data breaches globally, with 147.9 million U.S. consumers' data being stolen by cyber attackers. Initially, on September 7, 2017, Equifax disclosed the breach impacting 143 million consumers.[3]

Subsequently, it reported another 2.5 million consumers were impacted on October 2, 2017.[4]

Then, on March 1, 2018, Equifax disclosed it had discovered 2.4 million consumers whose names and partial driver's license information had also been stolen by the cyber attackers.[5]

Here are the key ways in which consumers were impacted by the Equifax data breach.

- ❑ The data stolen included social security numbers, birth dates, addresses, driver's license numbers, passport images and other personally identifiable information, involving 147.9 million U.S. consumers. This is the equivalent of nearly half the population of the U.S.

❑ The breach also involved the cyber attackers gaining access to data involving consumers in Canada and the U.K.

❑ The breach resulted in multiple lawsuits filed by consumers as well as regulators. Equifax agreed to settle the consolidated lawsuits for $700 million. The company estimates total breach costs will be over $1.7 billion.

Figure 1. Equifax timeline

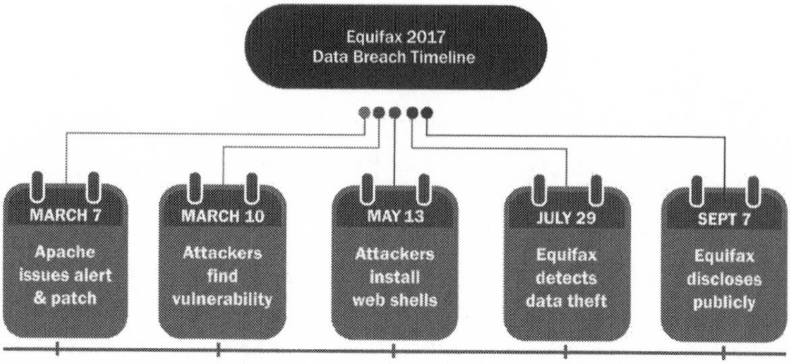

The sequence of events was as follows.

On March 7, 2017, the Apache Software Foundation issued an alert on an Apache Struts vulnerability. It also released the patch the same day. MITRE's CVE-2017-5638 with a CVSS score of 10 also alerted and made known publicly the critical rating of the vulnerability.[6] Apache Struts is an open-source software for creating enterprise-grade Java web applications and is used by hundreds of financial institutions, government organizations, technology providers and Fortune 100 companies.

On March 8, 2017, the U.S. Department of Homeland Security, Computer Emergency Readiness Team (U.S. CERT) sent Equifax and many others a notice reminding them of the need to patch the Apache Struts vulnerability.

In the meantime, cyber attackers ramped up efforts on the Internet to scan and identify companies and systems with the vulnerability to exploit.

On March 10, 2017, just three days after the Apache alert and CVE was made public, the cyber attackers found Equifax and identified that it was exposed to the Apache Struts vulnerability, according to Mandiant, the cybersecurity firm hired by Equifax to conduct a forensic review of the data breach.[7]

Then on May 13, 2017, the cyber attackers exploited the unpatched vulnerability to enter Equifax's network and started to insert web shells. In total, they inserted 30 web shells in Equifax's web pages; hidden pages that would allow remotely running commands on Equifax's systems. The cyber attackers then continued to move around laterally and found unencrypted application credentials (i.e. user names and passwords), which they used to gain access to 48 databases.[8]

The cyber attackers gained access to multiple tables and databases, including those that support Equifax's online consumer-dispute web application containing consumer data. They ran 9,000 queries, out of which 265 returned datasets containing consumers' personally identifiable information (PII). The attackers stored the PII datasets in compressed files in a web accessible directory. The attackers then used the web shells and 35 different IP addresses and encryption to transmit data for 147.9 million U.S. consumers, evading Equifax's detection. [9]

Equifax finally detected the breach on July 29, 2017 and realizing it was from the Apache Struts vulnerability, implemented the patch on July 30, 2017.[10]

Equifax became aware of the vulnerability via the Apache alert and also that the patch was available the same day on March 7, 2017. They were also reminded by U.S. CERT on March 8, 2017 of the urgent need to patch the vulnerability.

Equifax did not, however, implement the patch until July 30, 2017, and as a result, it remained exposed to the cyber attackers exploiting the vulnerability for months. The critical Apache Struts vulnerability with a CVSS score of 10 remained unpatched for 144 days.

According to testimony provided by the former Equifax CEO to lawmakers in the U.S. Congress, Equifax did circulate the U.S. CERT alert on March 9, 2017 to personnel reminding them of the need to patch the vulnerability promptly; however, the patch was not made.[11]

It was also reported that on March 15, 2017, an information security department scan failed to identify the unpatched vulnerability.[12]

Signals missed

The cyber attackers found Equifax exposed to the Apache Struts vulnerability on March 10, 2017, and on May 13, 2017, they exploited the unpatched vulnerability to enter Equifax's network. They remained undetected while moving around laterally and successfully getting to the **Crown Jewels** and stealing the data until July 30, 2017 when Equifax eliminated the attackers' access. The following are the signals that were missed by Equifax in the critical Cyber Attack Chain steps.

❑ **intrusion**
   The cyber attackers identified Equifax with the Apache Struts vulnerability, broke in and installed 30 web shells in Equifax web pages, providing signals.

❑ **lateral movement**
   The cyber attackers were able to move laterally undetected from May 13, 2017 to July 30, 2017. During this time, stealing the application credentials and the internal reconnaissance and movement to hunt for the tables and databases related to the online consumer-dispute web application provided signals. Also, running the 9,000 queries and storing the datasets in compressed files provided signals.

❑ **command and control**
   Prior to the start of the transmission of the consumer data out of Equifax using encryption, communications with the C&C servers to firm up the transmission provided signals. Also, the use of 35 different IP addresses signaled anomalous C&C communications.

Key takeaway lessons

Had Equifax implemented Cyber Attack Signals, the cyber attackers would most probably have been detected early and the data theft avoided.

❑ **intrusion**
The Cyber Attack Signal, patch window, would most probably have detected and highlighted the unpatched Apache Struts vulnerability, starting on March 7, 2017, as soon as the Apache alert and CVE with a CVSS score of 10 was issued. This vulnerability remained unpatched for 144 days. Another Cyber Attack Signal, web shell, would most probably have detected the 30 web shells installed by the cyber attackers on web pages to attack the **Crown Jewels**, such as the online consumer-dispute web application and related database.

❑ **lateral movement**
The Cyber Attack Signals, abnormal logons and privileged users' behavior, would most probably have detected the attackers using the stolen application credentials to access 48 databases, while internal reconnaissance signals, would most probably have detected cyber attackers' behavior when moving around the network multiple times and early on such as when running 9,000 queries or storing the datasets generated from the 265 queries in compressed files.

❑ **command and control**
The Cyber Attack Signal, C&C communications, would most probably have detected cyber attackers communications with the C&C servers to firm up the upcoming exfiltration of data. Hidden tunnels, also would most probably have signaled the cyber attackers getting ready to transmit the data using encryption.

While there were several signals missed by Equifax, the exploitation of the unpatched Apache Struts vulnerability by the cyber attackers was key to their success. Had Equifax implemented the Cyber Attack Signal (patch window), the unpatched vulnerability would have been highlighted and escalated, and the exposure would not have been allowed to remain open for so many days, providing the attackers with an entry point and a wide-open window.

The patch window would have highlighted not only each day the vulnerability remained unpatched, but also would have shed light on the specific Apache Struts vulnerability and how the attackers could exploit it, providing an alert as to which **Crown Jewels** were impacted and might be targets, the probable attack timeline and attackers' expected behavior as they tried to exploit the specific vulnerability.

The cyber attackers found Equifax exposed to the vulnerability on March 10, 2017, within three days of the vulnerability and patch being released publicly on March 7, 2017. Each day was a race against the cyber attackers and the patch window would have alerted senior management and board of directors at Equifax to oversee prompt risk mitigation.

Because the vulnerability remained unpatched, the attackers were able to exploit it and enter Equifax's network on May 13, 2017, after two months from the time the vulnerability was first made known publicly.

That is why the senior management and board of directors at every organization must implement Cyber Attack Signals, and as part of its early warning system, implement patch window. That will provide an early warning, and enable effective oversight and monitoring of timely remediation of critical vulnerabilities, a key cybersecurity risk and threat.

At Equifax, with a dashboard of Cyber Attack Signals, senior management and the board of directors could have asked management some key questions.

- ❑ Are all vulnerabilities in the scope of the patch window?
- ❑ How do we know for sure that any unpatched vulnerabilities have not been missed in the reporting of the patch window?
- ❑ Which vulnerabilities remain unpatched as reported in the patch window? Which **Crown Jewels** are impacted? What does the un-

patched vulnerability type tell us about the attackers' probable timeline, exploit method and the behavior to monitor for?

❑ Why could the patches not be implemented right away?

❑ How soon will the patches be implemented?

Five key takeaways from this chapter

❑ Most breaches occur because cyber attackers exploit vulnerabilities and break into the network before the vulnerabilities are either patched or before an interim workaround defense is implemented to keep the cyber attackers out, while the patch is being worked on.

❑ The Cyber Attack Signal, **patch window**, is the time period between a known vulnerability and the fix (i.e. the patch). It is the number of days a vulnerability remains unpatched, but also highlights the vulnerability type and how the attackers could exploit it, providing an alert into which **Crown Jewels** might be targets, the probable attack timeline and attackers' expected behavior.

❑ While there were several signals missed by Equifax, the exploitation of the unpatched Apache Struts vulnerability by the cyber attackers was key to their success. The Apache Struts vulnerability with a CVSS score of 10 remained unpatched for more than four and half months (144 days). Because the vulnerability remained unpatched, the attackers were able to exploit it and enter Equifax's network on May 13, 2017, after two months from the time the vulnerability was first made known publicly.

❑ Each day was a race against the cyber attackers and **patch window** would have alerted senior management and board of directors at Equifax to oversee prompt risk mitigation, including promptly identifying all **Crown Jewels** that might be targets because of the specific Apache Struts vulnerability, and expected attackers' behavior while attempting to exploit the vulnerability.

❑ While Equifax became aware of the Apache Struts vulnerability and circulated the security alert internally, this process was inadequate to properly managing cyber risk. It was missing a system of Cyber Attack Signals, including patch window, to detect, highlight and escalate the exposure. This would have enabled proper oversight from the highest levels to ensure prompt and complete risk mitigation.

Chapter 6

Anthem: Abnormal Logons

Chapter 6

Anthem: Abnormal Logons

The Anthem case was one of the largest data breaches in healthcare benefits globally, with 78.8 million U.S. consumers' data being stolen by cyber attackers.

Here are the key highlights of the Anthem data breach.

❑ Anthem (previously Wellpoint) is the largest healthcare benefits company by membership in the U.S.

❑ The data stolen included social security numbers, member ID numbers, healthcare ID numbers, birth dates, names, addresses, phone numbers and emails involving 78.8 million U.S. consumers.

❑ The breach involved the cyber attackers using phishing email to fool an Anthem user to click on the link in the email and download malware.

❑ Cyber attackers then gained remote access to the user's logon credentials and computer and used it to move laterally inside Anthem's network.

❑ The breach involved the cyber attackers using the initial entry to gain access to at least 50 user logon credentials and computers involving 90 systems and eventually gaining access to Anthem's enterprise data warehouse.

Figure 1. Anthem timeline

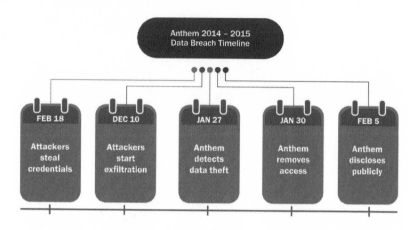

The sequence of events was as follows.[1]

On February 18, 2014, cyber attackers sent phishing emails to several Anthem employees and fooled one person to open it. It contained the malicious link. Opening this email and clicking on the link permitted the download of malware, a remote access trojan (RAT), to the employee's local system, allowing the cyber attackers to gain remote access to that computer and the employee's logon credentials.

Figure 2. Anthem flow

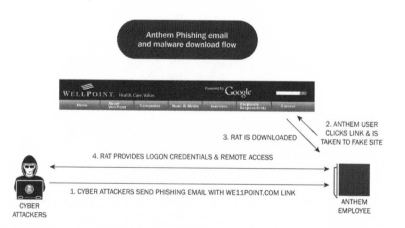

Figure 2 depicts the phishing email flow that took the user to we11point. com, a look alike Wellpoint IT site, to download the malware.

Starting with this initial remote access, over the next several months from mid-February to early December, the cyber attackers were able to move laterally across Anthem's systems undetected, obtain access to the other users' credentials and systems, and escalate privileges (i.e. gain greater ability to access information and make changes in Anthem's systems).

The cyber attackers gained access to at least 50 accounts and compromised 90 systems within the Anthem network, including, eventually, access to Anthem's **Crown Jewels**, the enterprise data warehouse (i.e. the database storing consumer information).

Then, on December 10, 2014, cyber attackers started running queries to the data warehouse to access the consumer information and start the exfiltration. On January 27, 2015, a database administrator at Anthem discovered that a data query was running using the employee's logon credentials. The employee immediately alerted Anthem's information security department. Anthem then notified the FBI about the potential breach, and initiated an internal investigation.

On January 30, 2015, Anthem terminated the attackers' access and exfiltration, but by that time the cyber attackers had successfully exfiltrated data involving 78.8 million U.S. consumers.

Then on February 5, 2015, Anthem announced publicly that it had suffered the data breach.[2] After the public disclosure, these events happened at Anthem:

- ❏ dozens of class-action lawsuits by consumer plaintiffs impacted by the data breach;
- ❏ multi-state insurance regulatory agency investigation;
- ❏ negative publicity.

Since the data breach, Anthem has invested significantly ($2.5 million for expert consultants, $115 million for cybersecurity improvements, $31 million for notice to affected consumers and $112 million for credit protection to impacted consumers) to boost its cybersecurity and resolved the multistate insurance regulatory agency investigation.[3] It has also obtained a consolidated class-action settlement involving the creation of a $115 million settlement fund.[4]

The key to the cyber attackers success was Anthem's inability to detect the signals of compromise of a large number of users' credentials (at least 50 users' credentials and accounts impacting 90 systems were compromised) over 11 months.

Cyber attackers know that traditional intrusion detection systems are focused on detecting anomalous network traffic, not necessarily anomalous logons into computers inside a network. Those systems generally are unable to discern from the traffic what is normal as opposed to what are malicious logons and therefore unable to detect the anomalous logons. Cyber attackers frequently exploit this exposure.

Once inside the network, the attackers focus on stealing credentials of one user then another to move laterally inside the network, hunting for the **Crown Jewels** to steal. The stolen logon credentials of the users provide the means for the cyber attackers to move laterally undetected.

Cyber attackers will also attempt to target users with privileged access levels (e.g. database administrative users) because their stolen logon credentials will provide greater capabilities to the chain of compromised computers and a faster path to reaching the **Crown Jewels**.

Figure 3. Abnormal logons

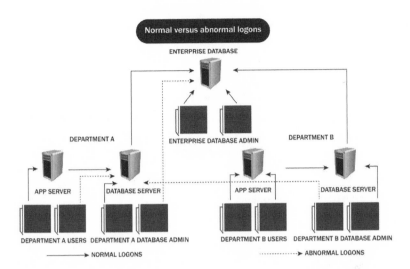

Figure 3 illustrates an example of normal versus abnormal logons inside a network.

The solid lines are normal logons by users or users with privileged credentials (e.g. database administrative users). The dashed lines are abnormal logons, such as these:

- ❑ logon attempt or logon by a user in Department A without privileged credentials into Department A database server;
- ❑ logon attempt or logon by a Department A database administrative user into the enterprise database server which is restricted normally only to enterprise database administrative users;
- ❑ logon attempt or logon by Department B database administrative user into Department A database server which is restricted normally only to Department A database administrative users.

Because cyber attackers have to use a stolen user's credentials to attempt the logon or logon to the next user's computer or a database, many of the logons will be abnormal compared to normal logons for the targeted users and computers. That is going to happen since the cyber attackers can only use what they have been able to steal up to that point in order to move forward. This provides the opportunity to detect the abnormal logons early on in the lateral movement as illustrated in the three examples in Figure 3.

Additionally, closely monitoring logons to the **Crown Jewels**, even by database administrative users or other privileged users with normal and expected access, to look for anomalies is critical. Database administrative users logons at an unusual time of day or night or performing unusual tasks, such as running large queries, is a sign of abnormal logons and early warning of compromised user credentials and the beginning of a data breach and exfiltration.

A key step is first to establish normal logon pattern thresholds in terms of user types, time, frequency, tasks, and source and destination, based on network logon history. Resolution of any anomalies detected should be in hours, not days or weeks. The normal logon patterns should be identified for both privileged users (e.g. database administrative users and others with privileged access) and regular users.

While the privileged users' credentials are inherently high risk for theft, regular user credentials are also at risk since they can provide the initial entry point or facilitate the lateral movement and chain of compromise of other users and computers. Once the normal logon patterns are determined, monitoring of abnormal logons can be activated for anomalies.

Extensive numbers of logons will most probably exist in any network in any time period given the nature of logons. Thus, an algorithm and tool will probably be necessary to automate the efficient and effective analysis of the logons to mine through the vast amount of logon data. This way, anomalies compared to normal patterns can be identified to trigger abnormal logons.

Signals missed

The cyber attackers initially broke into Anthem and gained a foothold on February 18, 2014, and remained undetected while moving around laterally and successfully getting to the **Crown Jewels** and stealing the data, until January 30, 2015, when Anthem eliminated the attackers' access. The following signals were missed by Anthem in the critical steps of the Cyber Attack Chain.

- ❏ **lateral movement**

  The cyber attackers were able to move laterally undetected for a period of more than 11 months. During this time period, multiple logon attempts using the stolen user credentials, involving at least 50 user accounts to logon to 90 systems, provided signals. In addition, reconnaissance to find Anthem's enterprise data warehouse, and then attempts to logon to the **Crown Jewels** using the stolen privileged users' credentials provided signals. Then, on December 10, 2014, the cyber attackers' running of queries to the data warehouse using stolen credentials provided further signals.

- ❏ **command and control**

  As malware was installed, communications with the C&C server provided signals.

Key takeaway lessons

Had Anthem implemented Cyber Attack Signals, the cyber attackers would most probably have been detected early and the data theft avoided.

- ❏ **lateral movement**

  The Cyber Attack Signals — abnormal logons, privileged users' behavior, internal reconnaissance signals and malware signals — would most probably have detected cyber attackers' behavior multiple times and early on during the period of more than 11 months. In particular, the abnormal logons, would most probably have detected the 50 user accounts' compromise involving 90 systems. The various signals would have provided Anthem with multiple opportunities to detect the cyber attackers early.

- ❏ **command and control**

  The Cyber Attack Signal, C&C communications, would most probably have detected cyber attackers' behavior prior to exfiltration. As malware was installed, communications with the C&C server provided signals.

The magnitude of the data breach at Anthem involving 78.8 million consumers illustrates what can happen when critical signals are not detected. That is why the senior management and board of directors at every organization must implement Cyber Attack Signals, and as part of its early warning system, implement abnormal logons. This will provide early warning and enable effective oversight and monitoring for timely detection of cyber attackers.

With a dashboard of Cyber Attack Signals, senior management and the board of directors at Anthem could have asked management key questions.

- ❑ Do abnormal logons cover all **Crown Jewels** and all users and the entire network or are there certain **Crown Jewels**, users, servers or parts of the network not covered in the scope?
- ❑ If certain users, servers or parts of the network are not covered in the scope, why not?
- ❑ Is an algorithm and tool used to mine logon data to identify anomalies and trigger abnormal logons?
- ❑ Does the Cyber Attack Signal, abnormal logons, not indicate anomalous behavior and what is status of investigation?
- ❑ What is the risk that cyber attackers are inside the network and using stolen user credentials and moving laterally to get to the **Crown Jewels**?

Five key takeaways from this chapter

- ❑ Once inside the network, the attackers steal credentials of one user then another to move laterally inside the network, hunting for the **Crown Jewels**. The stolen logon credentials provide the means for the cyber attackers to move laterally undetected. Cyber attackers also steal credentials of users with privileged access levels (e.g. database administrative users) because their stolen logon credentials provide greater capabilities to the chain

---

of compromised computers and a quicker path to reaching the **Crown Jewels**.

❏ Because cyber attackers have to use a stolen user's credentials to attempt the logon or logon to the next user's computer or a database, many of the **logons** will be **abnormal** compared to normal logons for the targeted users and computers. That is going to happen since the cyber attackers can only use what they have been able to steal up to that point in order to move forward.

❏ At Anthem, the cyber attackers were able to move laterally undetected for a period of more than 11 months. During this time period, multiple logon attempts using the stolen users' credentials, provided signals. In addition, reconnaissance to find Anthem's **Crown Jewels** (enterprise data warehouse) and attempts to logon using the stolen privileged users' credentials provided signals. The cyber attackers' running of queries to the data warehouse using stolen credentials provided further signals.

❏ The key to the cyber attackers' success was Anthem's inability to detect the signals of compromise of a large number of users' credentials (at least 50 user credentials and accounts impacting 90 systems were compromised.)

❏ The Cyber Attack Signals — abnormal logons, privileged users' behavior, internal reconnaissance signals and malware signals — would most probably have detected cyber attackers' behavior multiple times and early on during the period of more than 11 months. In particular, **abnormal logons** would most probably have detected the 50 user accounts' compromise involving 90 systems.

Chapter 7

U.S. OPM: Privileged Users' Behavior

Chapter 7

U.S. OPM: Privileged Users' Behavior

The U.S. Government's Office of Personnel Management (OPM) data breach is one of the largest in the government sector globally, with 21.5 million U.S. federal government employees, prospective employees, dependents and contractors data being stolen by cyber attackers.

Here are the key implications from the OPM data breach.

❑ The data stolen includes social security numbers, birth dates, names, addresses, phone numbers, emails and other personally identifiable information and background investigations data involving 21.5 million individuals, including the fingerprints data for 5.6 million individuals.[1]

❑ The breach has significant national security risk implications for the U.S. because the scope involved not only theft of data relating to federal government employees, but also prospective employees, dependents, contractors, and their detailed background information, passport images and fingerprints data.[2]

Figure 1. OPM timeline

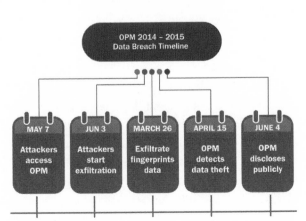

Figure 1 provides highlights of the OPM data breach timeline.[3]

It is important to note that OPM had suffered another data breach earlier on March 20, 2014, when the United States Computer Emergency Readiness Team (U.S. CERT) detected exfiltration of data by cyber attackers from OPM's network, involving manuals and IT systems architecture information, list of contractor employees, among other information.

Since the exfiltration did not involve personally identifiable information, however, such as social security numbers, usernames, passwords or background investigations information, OPM decided to monitor the cyber attackers activities for a period of time to learn details of the attack method, systems compromised, and identify all possible malware installed and command and control connections established.

OPM then worked with the U.S. CERT to plan for complete removal of the cyber attackers access on May 27, 2014, calling it the 'Big Bang' event.

OPM was able to eliminate cyber attackers' access on that day. While OPM was monitoring and planning for the May 27 event, however, the cyber attackers were able to gain access elsewhere in the network where OPM was not looking.

On May 7, 2014, cyber attackers used the stolen credentials of an employee with KeyPoint (a contractor firm hired by OPM to perform background investigations of employees and prospective employees of the federal government) to access OPM's network. This employee had credentials to access the OPM system remotely via a virtual private network (VPN) to upload background investigations data and perform other job related tasks.[4]

The cyber attackers built a virtual machine in a hosted server located in California that mimicked and looked like the contractor background investigator's laptop and using the stolen credentials of the contractor, accessed the OPM network via the VPN. Then once inside the network, the attackers started hunting for privileged users. There were at least 50 privileged users with network-administrator access credentials, according to testimony provided by OPM officials to lawmakers in the U.S. Congress.[5]

So the cyber attackers had to steal only one of the 50 privileged users' credentials to obtain the 'keys to the kingdom' and move laterally and obtain access to sensitive databases. After stealing privileged users' credentials, the cyber attackers then started moving laterally, found the database containing the background investigations and installed malware, and started exfiltration on June 3, 2014. Cyber attackers continued exfiltration of the data until August 2014.

Then on December 15, 2014, cyber attackers discovered the personnel files database and successfully exfiltrated additional data. Then on March 26, 2015, the attackers discovered fingerprints data and successfully exfiltrated this data relating to 5.6 million individuals.

On April 15, 2015, an OPM contractor employee discovered an unknown Secure Sockets Layer (SSL) certificate on the OPM network being used to encrypt communications with a malicious domain "opmsecurity.org". The next day, OPM staff detected malware beaconing out to a C&C server. The malware was a file called mcutil.dll acting as if it was a McAfee antivirus executable.

OPM, however, did not use McAfee, so it became evident it was a malware installed by the cyber attackers. That same day, on April 16, 2015, OPM notified U.S. CERT of the suspicious activity and requested a forensics examination.

On April 17, 2015, working with U.S. CERT, OPM eliminated the cyber attackers' access to the OPM network and started working to find and eliminate all malware that the cyber attackers may have installed.

On April 30, 2015, OPM notified the U.S. Congress of the data breach, and on June 4, 2015, OPM announced news of the data breach to the public.

After the public disclosure, these events happened at OPM:

- ❑ several U.S. congressional hearings on the impact from the data breach;
- ❑ an Office of Inspector General (OIG) investigation;
- ❑ negative publicity;

❏ a class-action lawsuit filed by the American Federation of Government Employees on behalf of the individuals impacted by the data breach;

❏ a demand from U.S. Congressional leaders for the resignation of OPM officials;

❏ the resignation of the OPM director, CIO and other officials.

While OPM could have implemented several measures that would have enhanced its cybersecurity and made it less vulnerable, such as limiting the number of privileged users with network administrator access from the 50 to a much smaller number, OPM did not detect abnormal behavior and the compromise of privileged users' credentials.

OPM should not only have been monitoring for any abnormal behavior of the privileged users, such as network administrators, but also should have considered all VPN access by contractor users as privileged users and monitored them, especially in light of the fact that cyber attackers had previously stolen the list of contractor employees with the March 2014 data breach. The contractors' credentials were inherently high risk because they provided a clear entry point into the OPM network and were susceptible to credential theft outside of OPM, which is what happened in this case.

By stealing the OPM contractor's user credentials outside of the OPM environment, the cyber attackers were able to enter the OPM network via the VPN by pretending to be the OPM contractor, and access the Windows Active Directory which by default provided read access to content, including a list of privileged users and groups in the network.

So very quickly the cyber attackers were able to identify all individuals with 'keys to the kingdom' and began targeting the privileged users to steal their credentials. Then, using the stolen privileged users' credentials, the cyber attackers gained access to the OPM SQL server and used remote desktop protocol (RDP) to install malware.

The OPM SQL server provided the pivot point for lateral movement, moving from computer to computer, system to system, into the **Crown Jewels** (i.e. the background investigations, fingerprints and personnel records systems and databases.)[6]

The cyber attackers had also installed a Secure Sockets Layer (SSL) certificate on the OPM network to encrypt C&C communications with the malicious domain "opmsecurity.org" and this remained undetected by OPM for several months and was only discovered by an OPM contractor manually instead of through automated monitoring and by that time it was too late.[7]

Signals missed

The cyber attackers initially broke in via the VPN and gained a foothold on May 7, 2014, using the stolen logon credentials of an OPM contractor with VPN access. Then once inside, the attackers hunted for privileged users in OPM's system and stole privileged users' credentials to move laterally inside OPM's network. They were successful in getting to the **Crown Jewels** and stealing the data until April 17, 2015, when OPM eliminated the attackers' access. The following are the signals that were missed by OPM in the critical Cyber Attack Chain steps:

❑ **lateral movement**
The cyber attackers were able to move laterally undetected for a period of more than 11 months. The initial entry via the VPN using the stolen OPM contractor credentials and lateral movement to hunt for privileged users' credentials (OPM had at least 50 users with network administrator privilege access), provided signals. During this time period, the internal reconnaissance for the privileged users and the **Crown Jewels**, provided signals. Installation of malware on servers, in particular, on the OPM SQL server, using remote desktop protocol (RDP) also provided signals.

❑ **command and control**
Prior to the beginning of the multiple transmission of the data out of OPM, communications with the C&C server to firm up the transmission provided signals. Periodic .dll file communication attempts with the C&C server provided signals. Encrypted com-

munications using unknown SSL certificate with domain "opmsecurity.org" also provided signals.

Key takeaway lessons

Had OPM implemented Cyber Attack Signals, the cyber attackers would most probably have been detected early and the data theft avoided:

❏ **lateral movement**
The Cyber Attack Signals, privileged users' behavior, internal reconnaissance signals, malware signals and RDP signals, would most probably have detected the cyber attackers' behavior when moving around the network multiple times and early on during the 11 month plus period.

❏ **command and control**
The Cyber Attack Signal, C&C communications, would most probably have detected the .dll file communication attempts with the C&C server, and also the cyber attackers' communications with the C&C server to firm up the multiple planned exfiltration of data. Additionally, hidden tunnels would most probably have detected the cyber attackers getting ready to transmit the data using encryption and the unknown SSL certificate "opmsecurity.org".

While there were several signals missed by OPM, the exploitation of privileged users' credentials by the cyber attackers was key to their success. Had OPM implemented the Cyber Attack Signal, privileged users' behavior, the cyber attackers would most probably have been detected early. The OPM had at least 50 users with network administrator access, providing the cyber attackers with a nest of 'keys to the kingdom' to steal from.

Since cyber attackers will lurk in the network for several months, looking for signals that cyber attackers have obtained the 'keys to the kingdom' as early on as possible is a key to timely detection.

Consider the value of privileged users' credentials to cyber attackers. Once cyber attackers gain access to the network, and it is only a matter of time, they will hunt for privileged users so they can steal their credentials. This is because the credentials of privileged users are more valuable than a regular user and provide the 'keys to the kingdom'.

Privileged users are those users with greater access levels and capabilities required for their jobs than a regular user, such as a network or database administrator with access to the network or database with certain capabilities required to perform their jobs.

Because of the greater access levels and capabilities these users possess, stealing their credentials provides a faster path to the **Crown Jewels**. For example, if cyber attackers steal the credentials of a database administrator who manages a database containing consumer data, they will immediately be able to access this database pretending to be the database administrator and start planning exfiltration of the data.

Because these privileged users possess greater access levels and capabilities, cyber attackers prioritize stealing their credentials so they can use them to get to the **Crown Jewels**. Sometimes stealing just one privileged user's credentials will be enough to get to the **Crown Jewels**. But more often, it requires either escalating the privileges of a stolen privileged user's credentials or stealing one and then stealing another with greater privileges in order to get eventually to the **Crown Jewels**.

Who should be considered privileged users?

Some of the obvious categories are these:

❑ **domain or network administrators**
These users have access to all workstations and servers in order to perform various administrator tasks, such as system configurations, set up of administrative accounts and domain groups.

❑ **application or database administrators**
These users have full access to a specific application and database in order to perform various administrator tasks, such as configuring a database and running queries.

❑ **local administrators**
These users have access to a particular server or workstation in order to perform various administrator tasks, such as maintenance, set up of user groups and access levels.

❑ **business privileged users**
These users have access to sensitive databases based on job responsibilities and in order to perform various tasks, such as report generating and management of sales, CRM, HR, finance or similar databases.

❑ **support privileged users**
These users have access to business privileged users workstations or access to sensitive databases to perform job responsibilities, such as executive assistants and help desk IT staff with remote access to workstations.

In addition to these types of users, vendor or contractor users with access into the network, even via a VPN, in order to perform their job responsibilities, should also be considered privileged users, regardless of administrator capabilities.

These users' credentials are inherently high risk due to susceptibility to theft outside of the organization, such as in the vendor's or contractor's own network, and since these stolen credentials provide the entry point for the cyber attackers to start the hunt for other privileged users' credentials.

Windows Active Directory (WAD) also represents an inherently high risk exposure to the theft of privileged users' credentials. That is because if the cyber attackers can get access to WAD via the theft of even a regular user's credentials, they can view in WAD who all of the privileged users are, what groups they belong to and the interconnectivities.

If they steal a privileged user's credentials in WAD they can then either escalate the privileges of that user or use those credentials to plan the theft of a higher-level privileged user's credentials and continue the journey to the **Crown Jewels**.

WAD administrator users, such as enterprise admins (EA), domain admins (DA), built-in administrators (BA) and schema admins (SA), who have significant permissions and capabilities, should be included in the scope of who should be considered privileged users.

Here, for example, are some of the significant capabilities of the DA in WAD:[8]

- ❑ add workstations to domain;
- ❑ adjust memory quotas for a process;
- ❑ allow logon through remote desktop services;
- ❑ manage backup files and directories;
- ❑ change the system time;
- ❑ change the time zone;
- ❑ create global objects;
- ❑ debug programs;
- ❑ enable computer and user accounts to be trusted for delegation;
- ❑ force shutdown from a remote system;
- ❑ impersonate a client after authentication;
- ❑ load and unload device drivers;
- ❑ log on as a batch job;
- ❑ manage auditing and security log;
- ❑ modify firmware environment values;
- ❑ profile system performance;
- ❑ remove computer from docking station;
- ❑ restore files and directories;
- ❑ shut down the system;
- ❑ take ownership of files or other objects.

The Cyber Attack Signal, privileged users' behavior, provides an early warning of lateral movement of cyber attackers inside the network involving stolen privileged users' credentials.

The magnitude of the data breach at OPM, involving not only 21.5 million individuals, but the type of individuals and the type of data involved (i.e. background investigations data relating to federal government employees and contractors and their families, passport images and fingerprints) had significant national-security risk implications for the U.S.

The OPM case illustrates the magnitude of what can happen when critical signals are not monitored for or are missed. That is why the senior management and board of directors at every organization must implement Cyber Attack Signals, and as part of its early warning system, implement privileged users' behavior. That will provide early warning and enable effective oversight and monitoring for timely detection of cyber attackers with stolen 'keys to the kingdom.'

A key step is firstly to develop an inventory and perform analysis of all privileged users. It should in particular include vendor and contractor users with access via VPN or other ways into the network or into WAD and all WAD administrator users, such as enterprise admins, domain admins, built-in administrators and schema admins, who have significant permissions and capabilities.

Additionally, for WAD, a permission analysis should be performed to identify non-privileged users who may for some reason have been provided administrative privileges, such as permission to read or write, replicate directory changes or change or reset passwords. Any non-privileged users with these administrative privileges should be investigated immediately because it may indicate compromise or even if justified, these users should be considered privileged.

Next, for each of the privileged users, it is important to determine normal behavior patterns in terms of user types, permissions, logon times, frequency, duration, tasks, source and destination, based on privilege level, role and job duties. Resolution of any anomalies detected should happen in a matter of hours, not days or weeks.

An algorithm and tool with activity-correlation capability will probably be necessary to automate the efficient and effective analysis of the privileged users' behaviors, and to mine through the vast amount of historical data to create normal and expected behavior, and to identify the anomalies compared to normal patterns, and to trigger the Cyber Attack Signal, privileged users' behavior.

The scope should include monitoring and triggering alerts for any WAD permissions changes, such as adding administrative privileges not previously granted, read, write, replicate directory changes, change/reset password and unusual behavior (e.g. clearing audit logs).

Here are some of the high-risk WAD event/activity codes and anomalies related to privileged users that should be monitored and correlated for triggering alerts:[9]

1102	audit log was cleared
4625	logon failure — user tried to logon outside his day of week or time of day restrictions or the user has not been granted this logon right at this machine
4670	permissions on an object were changed
4672	special privileges assigned to new logon
4673	a privileged service was called
4704	a user right was assigned
4724	an attempt was made to reset an account's password
4728	a member was added to a security-disabled global group
4738	a user account was changed
4964	special groups have been assigned to a new logon

With a dashboard of Cyber Attack Signals, senior management at OPM could have asked management these key questions.

❑ Does the Cyber Attack Signal, privileged users' behavior, cover all privileged users (including users who normally may not be considered privileged, such as contractors with VPN access)?

❑ Is the number of privileged users and the access privileges reasonable and justifiable?

❑ Does the scope of the monitoring include behavioral detection algorithms to detect anomalous behavior when generating privileged users' behavior?

❑ What is the status of investigations of anomalies detected in privileged users' behavior?

❑ What is the risk that cyber attackers are inside the network and moving laterally using stolen privileged users' credentials to get to the **Crown Jewels** or are already there and about to steal the data?

Five key takeaways from this chapter

❑ Once cyber attackers intrude, they will hunt for privileged users so they can steal their credentials. This is because the credentials of privileged users are more valuable than a regular user and provide the 'keys to the kingdom'.

❑ Privileged users are those users with greater access levels and capabilities required for their jobs than a regular user, such as a network or database administrator. Because of the greater access levels and capabilities these users possess, stealing their credentials provides a quicker path to the **Crown Jewels**.

❑ Sometimes stealing just one privileged user's credentials will be enough to get to the **Crown Jewels**. But more often, it requires either escalating the privileges of a stolen privileged user's credentials or stealing one and then stealing another with greater privileges in order to get eventually to the **Crown Jewels**.

❑ While there were several signals missed by OPM, the exploitation of privileged users' credentials by the cyber attackers was key to their success. Had OPM implemented the Cyber Attack Signal, privileged users' behavior, the cyber attackers would most probably have been detected early. OPM had at least 50 users with network administrator access, providing the cyber attackers with a nest of 'keys to the kingdom' to steal from.

❑ OPM also did not consider contractor employees with VPN access, such as the background investigators, to be privileged users, and did not monitor their behavior. The attackers stole

---

several documents months before this massive data theft, which included list of contractor employees and their details. That was a critical warning sign missed by OPM. The attackers targeted these contractor employees outside of OPM, eventually stole a contractor employee's credentials and used it to access the OPM network via the VPN. They then used it for lateral movement to hunt for privileged users' credentials. Defining privileged users properly, and then monitoring for anomalies using the Cyber Attack Signal, privileged users' behavior, is a highly effective way to detect cyber attackers early in the Cyber Attack Chain.

Chapter 8

NHS England: Ransomware Signals

Chapter 8
NHS England: Ransomware Signals

A critical cyber threat that every organization is susceptible to is ransomware. In essence, it is a type of malware that instead of enabling the exfiltration of the **Crown Jewels**, enables hijacking until a ransom is paid in Bitcoins, to hide the cyber attackers identity. With ransomware, no **Crown Jewels** are stolen and taken away, instead the **Crown Jewels** are taken over, completely controlled and locked down by the cyber attackers until the ransom is paid.

In fact, it is not necessarily the **Crown Jewels** that are attacked; it is anything of value that the cyber attackers can identify that the victim will be willing to pay a ransom for. The cyber attackers are beginning to ask themselves, "Why take all of the trouble to steal when it is much easier to hijack and disrupt operations?"

First, I will explain what ransomware is and how it is perpetrated. Then I will illustrate the significant impact it can have on any type of organization by covering the U.K.'s NHS England case, and then cover in detail how to look for signals of ransomware for timely risk mitigation.

Ransomware is malware that falls into these two main types.

❑ **locker**
This type of ransomware creates a new desktop and disables keyboard functionalities so that the user cannot access any data, files, computers or devices. It frequently will display a message that the user has committed copyright infringement or that a law-enforcement authority will issue a fine for criminal violations, and the user must make a payment. In most cases, the ransomware can be removed and the victim's desktop can be restored to its original state.

❑ **crypto**

This type of ransomware encrypts a victim's data and files using symmetric and asymmetric encryption and renders them unusable. It frequently will display a message that unless a payment is made by a deadline, the data and files will be rendered unusable permanently. Once the payment is made, the decryption key is provided to the victim. It can encrypt data or files in mapped or unmapped network drives and is frequently designed to infect across a network. It is also frequently designed to search for and delete any backup data or files. That way the victim cannot simply turn to the backup and be up and running.

While both types of ransomware are being perpetrated by cyber attackers, the rate of crypto ransomware is increasing because cyber attackers realize that many organizations would rather pay the ransom than be locked out from the data being encrypted without a decryption key and face hours, days or weeks of disruption in operations and suffer significant damages.

A variant of crypto ransomware, SamSam, was recently perpetrated against victims in several sectors in the U.S. and Canada, ranging from healthcare to cities and municipalities. According to a grand jury indictment filed by the U.S. Department of Justice on November 26, 2018, against two Iranian nationals, these cyber attackers hacked into more than 200 organizations, installed SamSam ransomware, and demanded ransom payments from the victims.

The attackers collected more than $6 million in ransom payments. The victims incurred additional losses estimated to exceed $30 million from loss of access to their data while the ransomware encrypted their data and locked them out.[1]

For example, the City of Atlanta fell victim to SamSam ransomware on March 22, 2018. While it did not pay the ransom of $51,000 in Bitcoin demanded by the cyber attackers, it estimated it suffered $17 million in financial damages.[2]

Another variant of crypto ransomware, NotPetya, perpetuated on June 27, 2017, illustrates the devastating impact that ransomware can have on any organization and the large financial damages that can be inflicted. It affected many organizations globally in a variety of sectors and caused financial damages estimated to be more than $10 billion, according to a U.S. White House assessment by former U.S. Homeland Security adviser focused on cybersecurity, Tom Bossert.[3]

According to the United States Computer Emergency Readiness Team (U.S. CERT), after analyzing the NotPetya ransomware, it attributed the ransomware to the Russian military. The cyber attackers first used a backdoor to compromise an accounting software provider based in Ukraine, M.E. Doc, and its development environment, starting on April 14, 2017. The attackers then used this backdoor to run arbitrary commands, exfiltrate files, and download and execute exploits on the update server, and then used this server to infiltrate thousands of M.E. Doc's customers' computers running the software on June 27, 2017, and spread the ransomware around the world.

NotPetya modifies the master boot record (MBR) to enable encryption of the master file table (MFT) and the original MBR, and then reboots the system.[4] It also searches for and encrypts certain files, such as .pdf, .xls, .xlsx, .zip, and .ppt. Once the files are encrypted, it then generates the following ransomware note for the user.

Ooops, your important files are encrypted.

If you see this text, then your files are no longer accessible, because they have been encrypted. Perhaps you are busy looking for a way to recover your files, but don't waste your time. Nobody can recover your files without our decryption service.

We guarantee that you can recover all your files safely and easily. All you need to do is submit the payment and purchase the decryption key.

Please follow the instructions:

1.   Send $300 worth of Bitcoin to following address:

2.   Send your Bitcoin wallet ID and personal installation key to e-mail
     Your personal installation key:

It also searches for backup files to encrypt and various logs (such as the system, security and application logs) to clear out to avoid detection and hinder forensics.

NotPetya appeared to be similar to other types of crypto ransomware and generated a ransom note for the victim that said that the decryption key would be provided once the $300 Bitcoin payment was made. Because the ransomware irreversibly encrypted the computer's master boot records, however, it appears the cyber attackers never were after a ransom but instead wanted to destroy files, disrupt operations, and cause significant financial damage.

The following are some of the victims of NotPetya in various sectors and the financial damages suffered as reported publicly by these organizations:

- ❑ Merck, U.S., Pharmaceutical, $870 million
- ❑ FedEx, U.S., Transportation, $400 million
- ❑ Saint-Gobain, France, Construction, $384 million
- ❑ Maersk, Denmark, Shipping, $300 million
- ❑ Mondelez, U.S., Food, $188 million
- ❑ Reckitt Benckiser, U.K., Consumer Goods, $129 million

Merck is one of the largest biopharmaceutical companies in the world with more than $40 billion in revenues. It focuses on developing medicines and vaccines to improve human and animal health. In its case, the NotPetya ransomware caused significant disruption to manufacturing, research and development, daily operations and drug sales, totaling $870 million in financial damages.

The following is the breakdown of the $870 million financial impact from the NotPetya ransomware per the company's annual report, SEC Form 10-K:[5]

- ❑ $260 million — production shutdown leading to inability to fulfill orders and loss of drug sales.
- ❑ $285 million — manufacturing expense variances and cyber attack remediation expenses.
- ❑ $125 million — expenses for borrowing the GARDASIL9 vaccine that prevents certain cancer and diseases caused by Human Papillomavirus, from the U.S. Centers for Disease Control stockpile, due to production shutdown.

❑ $200 million — loss of drug sales due to residual backlog of orders.

In summary, NotPetya was a variant of crypto ransomware that was exploited by the Russian military, with significant financial impact to victim organizations. It reflects the risk that crypto ransomware poses to all organizations around the world.

Crypto ransomware is perpetrated by cyber attackers using dual encryption (i.e. symmetric and asymmetric). It generates the symmetric key (private key) locally using the victim's computer, and then uses it to encrypt the files. It then generates the asymmetric key (public key) to protect the symmetric key. The asymmetric key is generated either locally on the victim's computer or remotely on the cyber attackers C&C server.

Either way, the ransomware requires communication with the cyber attackers C&C server and uses the private and public key pairs for each victim to make sure that once the ransom is paid the public key cannot be used to decrypt files on other victims' computers infected using the same public key. It is always the unique private-public pair required to decrypt the encryption of files in a victim's computer.

Figure 1. Typical flow

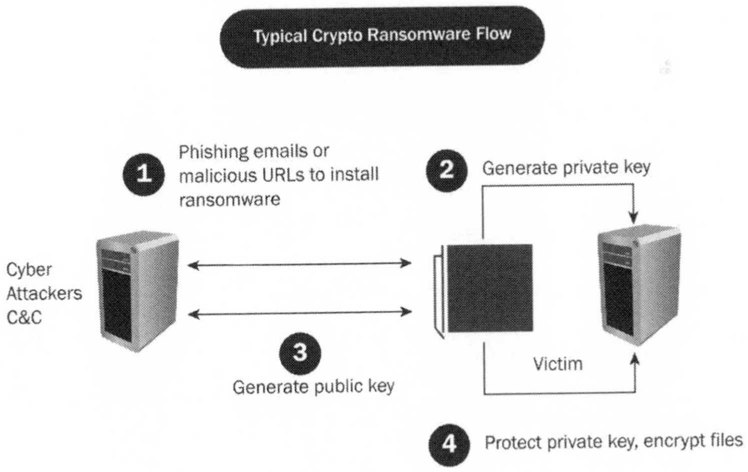

Figure 1 depicts a typical flow of how crypto ransomware is perpetrated by cyber attackers where the public key is generated at the cyber attackers C&C server.

The crypto ransomware is frequently customized to search for specific types of files or directories to encrypt that will have greater impact on the victim. It is also customized to search for and encrypt backup files and search for other users and computers to infect in the network.

Cyber attackers sometimes will use ransomware as a decoy and fake the victim for a more malicious attack, such as with a wiper malware, which wipes out data. The attackers will make it look like they have locked the victim out from accessing data or files using encryption and they will provide the decryption key once the ransom is paid. In the meantime, however, they will actually wipe out the data.

While instances of ransomware continue to remain highest in the U.S., other countries, including Brazil, Canada, China, Germany, India, Italy, Japan and the U.K., are also facing increased ransomware attacks. No country is immune to ransomware attacks.

The **WannaCry** (also known as WCry, WanaCrypt, and Wana Decrypt0r) ransomware was perpetrated on May 12, 2017. Although it was not the typical ransomware and was fortunately shut down quickly, it illustrates the potentially devastating impact that ransomware can have on any type of organization anywhere in the world.

Here is why WannaCry was a global threat and could have caused not just significant financial losses, but could have caused loss of human life, to illustrate the wide exposure that exists from ransomware, that every organization faces.

These were the key features of WannaCry:

❑ The ransomware was in the form of a worm, and was designed to target organizations that had not yet implemented the patch to vulnerabilities in Windows relating to Microsoft Windows Server Message Block (SMB) protocol.

❑ Microsoft had made the vulnerabilities known via Security Bulletin MS17-010 and made the patch available on March 14, 2017. MITRE's Common Vulnerabilities and Exposures also published on March 16, 2017 the CVEs 2017-0143, 2017-0144, 2017-0145, 2017-0146 and 2017-0148 with a rating of critical and a CVSS score of 9.3, and yet many organizations worldwide did not implement the patch promptly and remained exposed.[6,7]

❑ The ransomware was first reported at 4 a.m. EDT on May 12, 2017. It affected organizations of all sizes and types in more than 150 countries. It was designed to run in 27 different languages.[8]

❑ WannaCry was designed to spread to any unpatched computers on the network and to other exposed computers connected to the Internet. Within hours of its release on May 12, 2017, the worm had infected thousands of computers globally.

❑ It did not exfiltrate any data, but instead encrypted files to cut off access and disrupted operations. The worm targeted, searched for, and encrypted productivity, multimedia and database application files in order to disrupt operations, such as the following file extensions: .backup, .txt, .doc, .docx, .pdf, .xls, .xlsx, .zip, .ppt, .vbs, .jsp, .php, .java, .mp4, .wb2, and .db.

❑ The ransomware used a customized encryption protocol via TCP port 80 to connect to a C&C server to transmit the encryption keys.

❑ Once the files were encrypted on the victim's computer, WannaCry displayed the following ransom message with a timer and deadlines, threatening either the doubling of the ransom amount, if not paid in three days, or the permanent loss of files if not paid in seven days.

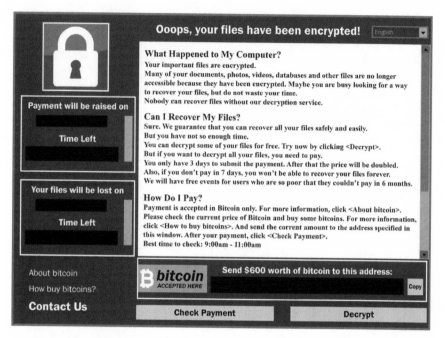

❑ The cyber attackers included a 'kill switch' in the ransomware. That directed the worm to connect to a hard-coded domain, which had not yet been activated. If the worm was not able to connect, it was to continue the encryption of files and propagate. If, however, it was able to connect, the worm was directed to stop encrypting files. Presumably, this was the method for the cyber attackers to stop the attack once ransoms had been paid, by activating the hard-coded domain.

❑ This 'kill switch' was discovered by a security researcher on the same day (May 12, 2017), and he was able to register it quickly, activate the hard-coded domain, and stop the ransomware from propagating further. Fortunately for the discovery of the 'kill switch', only approximately $140,000 in ransom had been paid by this time, but more importantly, no lives were lost. If this discovery had not been made the same day, not only millions could have been made by the cyber attackers, but they may have caused deaths.

This was the impact from WannaCry on the National Health Service (NHS) England in the United Kingdom (U.K.). It was one example of the hundreds of organizations impacted globally by the ransomware.

NHS England is one of four public health services organizations in the U.K. These healthcare organizations are comprised of trusts (i.e. groups of hospitals), general practitioners' (GP) practices and other healthcare providers.

Figure 2. NHS England timeline

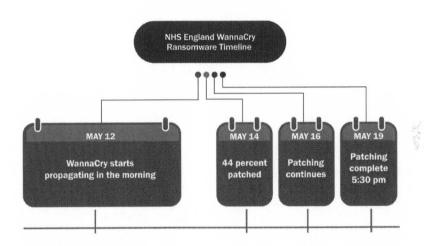

Figure 2 depicts the timeline of WannaCry followed by highlights of how the ransomware impacted NHS England and the close call it had in terms of potential loss of life.[9]

WannaCry started propagating early morning on Friday, May 12, 2017. Then late morning, several trusts in NHS England started reporting problems with their computers and unable to perform daily operations. While WannaCry was fortunately shut down by evening the same day, with the discovery of the 'kill switch' by the security researcher, the following impact had already occurred by this time at NHS England.

❏ 80 (34 percent) out of the 236 trusts were either infected by the ransomware and locked out or turned off their computers and devices or systems as a precaution. 34 of the 80 were locked out of their devices, of which 25 (74 percent) were acute trusts.

❑ Being locked out of devices prevented or delayed accessing and updating patient information, sending test results to GPs or transferring or discharging patients from the hospital. Being locked out of medical equipment and devices or turning off the devices as a precaution to prevent them being locked resulted in disruptions, such as in the radiology and pathology departments that rely on equipment and devices for diagnostic imaging (including MRI scanners) and for testing blood and tissue samples.

❑ Five trusts were unable to provide emergency care and had to divert ambulance services and patients to other hospitals.

❑ 603 primary care and other healthcare providers, including 595 GP practices, were infected with the ransomware.

❑ 6,912 appointments, including operations, were cancelled. Of those, 139 patients had urgent cancer referrals. NHS England estimated that 19,494 appointments would have been cancelled in total, based on the normal rate of follow-up to first appointments.

❑ 1,220 pieces of diagnostic equipment were infected. That impacted services, such as not being able to send MRI scan results to healthcare providers treating patients.

No ransom was paid by any of the NHS England organizations. While the cost of the WannaCry impact have not been calculated by NHS England, the financial impact is substantial and cost calculations will have to include not only costs from cancelled appointments and disruptions of operations, but the costs of staff overtime, consultants and IT resources required to assist with response and restoring data and systems affected by the ransomware.

Beyond the cost, what was fortunately avoided was a loss of life. While all of the impact to patients affected by the WannaCry disruptions have not been compiled and no loss of life has been reported, it was a close call.

We can imagine what could have happened, if one or more patients requiring emergency care had to be diverted from one of the five trusts, because they could not provide services due to the WannaCry impact, had a medical complication during transit to another facility, and died on the way or by the time they arrived at the diverted facility, it was too late.

Or let us imagine if the security researcher had not discovered the 'kill switch' that evening on May 12, 2017 and did not discover it until much later or not at all. The infection could have spread further through NHS England and impacted patients even more severely, leading to possible deaths.

NHS England was not specifically targeted by the cyber attackers with WannaCry but fell victim to the ransomware as did thousands of other organizations of all types and sizes in more than 150 countries. WannaCry copycats and other ransomware (e.g. Cerber, Locky, Mamba, SamSam and Spora) continue to be perpetrated globally and organizations of all types and sizes continue to fall victim.

Signals missed

The Windows SMB vulnerabilities were made known starting on March 14, 2017 by Microsoft. MITRE's CVEs highlighted the critical rating and the urgency to patch the vulnerabilities. Yet many organizations, including NHS England, did not patch the vulnerabilities and remained exposed for two months until the cyber attackers struck with the ransomware on May 12, 2017. The following are the signals that were missed by NHS England and other organizations that fell victim to the ransomware in the critical steps of the Cyber Attack Chain.

❏ **intrusion**
   The cyber attackers exploited the unpatched SMB vulnerabilities to break in. There was an early warning from the SMB vulnerability remaining unpatched.

❏ **lateral movement**
   The cyber attackers were able to install the ransomware quickly, exploiting the SMB vulnerabilities, and to spread the infection to

unpatched workstations and servers, providing signals. The worm also targeted, searched for, and encrypted productivity, multimedia and database application files in order to disrupt operations, providing signals as it spread.

❑ **command and control**
The ransomware used a customized encryption protocol via TCP port 80 to connect to a C&C server to transmit the encryption keys, providing signals.

Key takeaway lessons

Had NHS England implemented Cyber Attack Signals, the cyber attackers would most probably have been prevented from exploiting the vulnerabilities and the ransomware avoided or detected promptly.

❑ **intrusion**
The Cyber Attack Signal, patch window, would most probably have detected, highlighted, and escalated the unpatched SMB vulnerabilities as soon as the vulnerabilities were made known publicly. This vulnerability remained unpatched for two months.

❑ **lateral movement**
The Cyber Attack Signal, ransomware signals, would most probably have detected cyber attackers' behavior as soon the ransomware was installed and attempting to spread. The Cyber Attack Signal, SMB anomalies, would most probably also have detected the attempted exploitation of SMB vulnerabilities.

❑ **command and control**
The Cyber Attack Signals, C&C communications and hidden tunnels, would most probably have detected the cyber attackers' encrypted communications with the C&C server via TCP port 80 to transmit the encryption keys.

While there were several signals missed by NHS England, the exploitation of the unpatched SMB vulnerabilities by the cyber attackers was a key to their success. Had NHS England implemented the Cyber Attack Signal, patch window, the unpatched vulnerability would most probably have been highlighted and escalated right away, and the exposure would not have been allowed to remain open for two months for the attackers to take advantage of.

Ransomware signals would most probably also have provided signals of cyber attackers' behavior as soon as the ransomware was being installed and attempting to propagate to workstations and servers.

In addition to timely patching of vulnerabilities and implementing the patch window, the key is to monitor for signals of cyber attackers' behavior indicating either the first instance or very early instances of ransomware installation so as to allow for timely response in order to prevent spreading of the infection and any systemic impact. With ransomware signals, an organization can look for ransomware early on and prevent a ransomware epidemic.

While there are many variants of ransomware that an organization is susceptible to, there are certain behaviors that the cyber attackers and the ransomware will most probably exhibit that every organization should understand in order to effectively devise and implement ransomware signals.

Here are certain behaviors that may exhibit early signs of ransomware being installed or activated before widespread systemic impact:

- ❏ installation of a new .dll file;
- ❏ running a PowerShell command to connect to a TOR anonymization website;
- ❏ installation of TOR network anonymity software in TaskData folder with file named as .exe (e.g. taskhsvc.exe);
- ❏ creation of several new files .pky (public encryption key), .res (Command and Control communications), .eky (private encryption key);
- ❏ deletion of backup files (e.g. in shared network drive);
- ❏ renaming of productivity files (e.g. .doc, .pdf. and .xls);
- ❏ modifying Windows registry (e.g. modifying registry keys or system files).

An algorithm and tool with behavioral activity correlation capability will probably be necessary to automate the efficient and effective analysis of anomalous behaviors, and to mine through the vast amount of activity data, and to identify the anomalies and trigger the Cyber Attack Signal, ransomware signals. In all instances, investigation and resolution of the ransomware signals should occur within risk thresholds; but should be immediate.

With a dashboard of Cyber Attack Signals, senior management and board of directors at the NHS, including NHS England or other organizations, could have asked management these key questions:

- ❑ Which vulnerabilities remain unpatched in relation to the patch window? What **Crown Jewels** are impacted? What does the unpatched vulnerability type tell us about the attackers' probable timeline, exploit method and the behavior to monitor for?
- ❑ Why were the patches not able to be implemented right away and how soon will the patches be implemented?
- ❑ Do ransomware signals use behavioral detection algorithms and cover a comprehensive list of behaviors that may indicate ransomware?
- ❑ What is the status of investigations of anomalies indicated in ransomware signals?
- ❑ How can the organization use ransomware signals to detect ransomware early and prevent an epidemic?

Five key takeaways from this chapter

- ❑ **Ransomware** falls into these two main types: locker and crypto. While both types of ransomware are being perpetrated by cyber attackers, crypto ransomware and its variants are increasing because cyber attackers realize that many organizations would rather pay the ransom than be locked out from the data being encrypted without a decryption key and have to face hours, days or weeks of disruption in operations, and suffer significant damages.

❑ These two examples illustrate the devastating impact that ransomware can have on any organization and the large financial damages that can be inflicted:

  ○ **NotPetya**
  It affected many organizations globally in a variety of sectors, and caused financial damages estimated to be more than $10 billion.

  ○ **SamSam**
  It was perpetrated in several sectors in the U.S. and Canada, ranging from healthcare to cities and municipalities, where attackers hacked into more than 200 organizations, and installed the ransomware. The attackers collected more than $6 million in ransom payments. The victims incurred additional losses estimated to exceed $30 million from loss of access to their data.

❑ While there were several signals missed by NHS England, the exploitation of the unpatched SMB vulnerabilities by the cyber attackers was a key to their success. The Windows SMB vulnerabilities were made known by Microsoft and MITRE's CVEs highlighted the critical rating and the urgency to patch the vulnerabilities, and yet many organizations, including NHS England, did not patch the vulnerabilities and remained exposed for two months until the cyber attackers struck with the ransomware.

❑ Had NHS England implemented the cyberattack signal, **patch window**, the unpatched vulnerability would most probably have been highlighted and escalated right away, and the exposure would not have been allowed to remain open for two months for the attackers to take advantage of. **SMB anomalies** and **ransomware signals**, would most probably also have provided signals of the cyber attackers' behavior as soon as the ransomware was being installed and attempting to propagate to workstations and servers.

❑ In addition to timely patching of vulnerabilities and implementing the patch window, the key is to monitor for signals of cyber attackers' behavior, indicating either *the* first instance or very early instances of ransomware installation, so as to be able to make a timely response in order to prevent spreading of the infection and any systemic impact. With **ransomware signals**, an organization can detect signals of ransomware early on and prevent a ransomware epidemic.

Chapter 9

U.S. DNC: Unusual Logs Behavior

Chapter 9

U.S. DNC: Unusual Logs Behavior

The cyber attack on the U.S. Democratic National Committee (DNC) in 2016, also included hacking into the U.S. presidential campaign of Hillary Clinton and the Democratic Congressional Campaign Committee (DCCC), as described in the U.S. Department of Justice (DOJ) Indictment filed on July 13, 2018 by DOJ special counsel Robert Mueller against 12 Russian military intelligence officers.[1]

The indictment described how the cyber attacks were perpetrated to steal more than 50,000 emails and documents and how the data was released during the U.S. presidential elections in an attempt to influence the elections held in November 2016.

The cyber attack's scope also included the theft of donor records and personal identifying information of more than 2,000 Democratic donors, and attacks into various state election-related websites, including the theft of registration information (including names, addresses, partial social security numbers, dates of birth and driver's license numbers) for more than 500,000 voters from the website of a state board of elections.

It illustrates the extent of cyber risk and how it exists even in politics and how nations can try to influence elections in another country remotely with cyber attacks.

Figure 1. DNC timeline

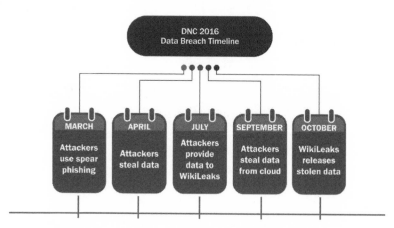

Figure 1 depicts the timeline of the DNC data breach.

Starting in March 2016, the cyber attackers targeted more than 300 individuals within the Clinton campaign, DCCC and DNC, and used spear phishing emails (targeted emails). The chairman of the Clinton campaign was one of the targets. The attackers created and sent a spear phishing email to the chairman, making it look like it was a security notification from Google asking him to change his password by clicking an embedded link. The link was to a fake website.

Unfortunately, the chairman fell victim and the attackers stole the chairman's credentials. Through other spear phishing emails, the attackers successfully stole credentials and thousands of emails from numerous other individuals with the Clinton campaign.

In April 2016, the attackers created an email account in the name (with a one-letter deviation from the actual spelling) of a known member of the Clinton campaign. The attackers then used that account to send spear phishing emails to the work accounts of many different Clinton campaign and DCCC employees. The spear phishing emails had an embedded link to a document named hillary-clinton-favorable-rating.xlsx. With this spear phishing, the attackers were able to steal the credentials of a DCCC employee, and gained access to the DCCC network.

Once they gained access, the attackers installed malware on DCCC computers, which allowed them to monitor individual employees' computer activity, steal passwords, and maintain access to the DCCC network. The malware captured keystrokes entered by DCCC employees, took screen shots of the computer screens, and transmitted the information from the victims' computers to the attackers' leased server in Arizona.

Subsequently, the attackers set up communication from the leased server to an overseas server, and then configured it remotely, and did a test to confirm that the malware could also directly communicate from a compromised DCCC computer with the overseas server.

The attackers were then able to use the malware to steal the credentials of a DCCC employee who had access to the DNC network. With the stolen credentials, the attackers hacked into the DNC network. The attackers then installed different types of malware, including some of the same as installed in the DCCC network and continued to collect thousands of keystroke captures and screen shots, and to steal other DNC employee credentials.

The attackers moved laterally to hunt for computers within the DCCC and DNC networks that stored information related to the 2016 U.S. presidential election. For example, the attackers searched one hacked DCCC computer for terms that included "hillary", "cruz" and "trump". The attackers also copied select DCCC folders, including "Benghazi Investigations". The attackers also targeted computers containing information, such as opposition research and field operation plans for the 2016 elections.

To enable them to steal a large number of documents at once without detection, the attackers used a publicly available tool to gather and compress multiple documents on the DCCC and DNC networks. The attackers then used malware to move the stolen documents outside the DCCC and DNC networks through encrypted channels.

For example, the attackers compressed gigabytes of data from DNC computers, including opposition research, and moved the compressed DNC data using malware to a leased computer located in Illinois. Later that day, the attackers used malware to connect to that computer to steal additional documents from the DCCC network.

Between May and June 2016, the attackers hacked the DNC Microsoft Exchange server and stole thousands of emails from the work accounts of DNC employees. During that time, the attackers researched PowerShell commands related to accessing and managing the Microsoft Exchange server.

During the lateral movement inside the networks, the attackers worked hard to cover their tracks by deleting logs and computer files. For example, in May 2016, the attackers cleared the event logs from a DNC computer, and in June 2016, the attackers deleted logs from the leased server in Arizona, including the login history. They also attempted to delete traces of their presence on the DCCC network using a program called CCleaner.

Despite the attackers efforts to hide, beginning in May 2016, both the DCCC and DNC became aware that they had been hacked, and hired a cybersecurity company to identify the extent of the intrusions. While the cybersecurity company took steps to shut down the attackers' access from the networks, a Linux-based version of the attackers' malware, programmed to communicate with the attackers' registered domain linuxkrnl.net, remained on the DNC network until October 2016.

Then in June 2016, the attackers registered a website DCLeaks and released some of the stolen emails and documents. At this point the DNC announced publicly that it had been hacked by Russian government actors. Before it was shut down in March 2017, the DCLeaks website had received more than one million page views.

Also in June 2016, at approximately the same time that the dcleaks.com website was launched, the attackers created a DCLeaks Facebook page, using a preexisting social media account under the fictitious name Alice Donovan. In addition to the DCLeaks Facebook page, the attackers used other social media accounts in the names of fictitious U.S. persons, such as Jason Scott and Richard Gingrey, to promote the DCLeaks website. The attackers also created the Twitter account @dcleaks.

In response to the DNC's announcement that it had been hacked by Russian government actors, the attackers created the online persona Guccifer 2.0 and falsely claimed to be a lone Romanian hacker to undermine allegations of Russian government involvement. The attackers then used Guccifer 2.0 to release documents stolen from the DCCC and DNC. In late June 2016, the attackers, posing as Guccifer 2.0, sent WikiLeaks an email with an attachment titled "wk dnc link1.txt.gpg."

While the DOJ indictment document refers to this organization as "Organization 1", the U.S. intelligence community in its declassified report *Assessing Russian Activities and Intentions in Recent U.S. Elections* stated, with a high degree of confidence, that it was WikiLeaks that the Russian government actors provided the stolen information to.[2] Several media sources, including a non-denial by WikiLeaks founder Julian Assange in an interview with CNN, have also reported that "Organization 1" was WikiLeaks.[3]

The attackers explained in the email to WikiLeaks that the encrypted file contained instructions on how to access an online archive of stolen DNC documents. On or about July 18, 2016, WikiLeaks, confirmed it had "the 1Gb or so archive" and would make a release of the stolen documents "this week." Then on July 22, 2016, WikiLeaks, released more than 20,000 emails and other documents stolen from the DNC network by the attackers. This release occurred approximately three days before the start of the Democratic National Convention. WikiLeaks did not disclose Guccifer 2.0's role in providing the stolen documents.

In July 2016, the attackers also hacked into the website of a state board of elections and stole information of approximately 500,000 voters, including names, addresses, partial social security numbers, dates of birth, and driver's license numbers.

The attackers, posing as Guccifer 2.0, also shared the stolen documents with certain individuals.

For example, in August 2016, posing as Guccifer 2.0, the attackers transferred approximately 2.5 gigabytes of data stolen from the DCCC to a lobbyist and online source of political news. The stolen data included donor records and personal identifying information of more than 2,000 Democratic donors.

In September 2016, the attackers successfully gained access to DNC computers hosted on a third-party cloud-computing service. These computers contained test applications related to the DNC's analytics. After conducting reconnaissance, the attackers gathered data by creating backups, or "snapshots," of the DNC's cloud-based systems using the cloud provider's own technology. The attackers then moved the snapshots to cloud-based accounts they had registered with the same service, thereby stealing the data from the DNC.

In order to expand their interference in the 2016 U.S. presidential election, the attackers transferred many of the documents they stole from the DNC and the chairman of the Clinton campaign to WikiLeaks. The attackers, posing as Guccifer 2.0, discussed the release of the stolen documents and the timing of those releases with WikiLeaks to heighten their impact on the 2016 U.S. presidential election.

In October 7, 2016, WikiLeaks released the first set of emails from the chairman of the Clinton campaign that had been stolen by the attackers. Then between October 7, 2016 and November 7, 2016, WikiLeaks released approximately thirty-three tranches of documents that had been stolen from the chairman of the Clinton campaign.

In total, more than 50,000 stolen emails and documents were released.

Signals missed

The cyber attackers used a variety of tactics, techniques and procedures (TTPs) to hack into the Clinton campaign, DCCC and DNC network in order to steal emails and documents. The following signals were missed by these related organizations in the critical steps of the Cyber Attack Chain:

❑ **lateral movement**
The cyber attackers were able to use spear phishing to steal credentials. They then used the stolen credentials to continue compromising other users and computers, and access and transmit out

emails and documents. The use of stolen credentials of users and privileged users provided multiple signals. The attackers also installed a variety of malware, providing many signals. The attackers also moved laterally and performed internal reconnaissance and worked hard to hide by deleting logs, providing many signals.

❑ **command and control**

The attackers used a variety of malware, which regularly communicated with the attackers' servers domestically and overseas, providing signals. The attackers also used encrypted channel for communications and transmission of stolen emails and documents, providing signals prior to transmission.

Key takeaway lessons

Had the Clinton campaign, DCCC and DNC implemented Cyber Attack Signals, the cyber attackers would most probably have been detected early and the data theft avoided. Another key takeaway is that the cloud is not immune to a data breach. The email and documents stored on the premises, along with the analytics database in the cloud, were equally susceptible and the attackers stole data from both using common TTPs, so the Cyber Attack Signals were necessary for monitoring both on the premises and in the cloud.

❑ **lateral movement**

The Cyber Attack Signals, abnormal logons and privileged users' behavior, would most probably have detected the widespread stealing of credentials and attempts to access the **Crown Jewels**. For example, the chairman of the Clinton campaign would have been identified as a privileged user and the signal, privileged users' behavior, would have monitored for anomalies and detected the attempted theft of the 50,000 emails from the chairman's account prior to exfiltration.

Internal reconnaissance signals would most probably also have detected the cyber attackers' behavior when moving around the network multiple times and early on. Additionally, malware signals would most probably have detected the widespread installation and infection, while malicious PowerShell would most probably have detected the use by the attackers when attempting to hack into the Microsoft Exchange server.

The Cyber Attack Signal, unusual logs behavior, would most probably have detected the clearing and deletion of the logs by the attackers. The attackers made a lot of effort to clear and delete logs in order to hide, so the signal was key to timely detection.

❑ **command and control**
The Cyber Attack Signal, C&C communications, would most probably have detected the many communications from the malware installed widely in the network — in both the lateral movement and the command and control steps in the Cyber Attack Chain — with the domestic and overseas servers prior to the upcoming exfiltration of data. The signal, hidden tunnels, would most probably also have signaled the cyber attackers getting ready to transmit the data using encryption.

As described in the indictment, one of the key signals was the clearing and deletion of logs during lateral movement by the cyber attackers to hide their trail. If the Cyber Attack Signal, unusual logs behavior, had been implemented, the cyber attackers would most probably have been detected in a timely manner.

While the configuration of a network that is targeted by cyber attackers will vary depending on the organization, there will be some common patterns in the attack methods, and event logs can provide critical signals and evidence.[4]

An event log captures and stores critical traffic, usage and behavior data about a network, users, system (such as Windows) or application. This data includes information, such as user logon sessions, account lockouts, failed password attempts, process start or end, application errors and closures. Cyber attackers will frequently either remove, stop or clear event logs in order to prevent detection, and to destroy evidence of the cyber attack.

Monitoring should be implemented, and an alert should be triggered if any event logs, such as in Microsoft Windows, the system, security, terminal services and audit logs, are removed, stopped or cleared. For example, in Windows, the cyber attackers can remove event logs via the wevtutil command or stop the log service via Invoke-Phantom0m or clear the event logs via tools such as Mimikatz.

A Cyber Attack Signal that summarizes the alerts generated indicating any event logs removed, stopped or cleared with details, such as user details, date, time, type of log, command executed to impact the event log, **Crown Jewels** or other asset impacted, source and destination, will provide a signal that it is most probably cyber attackers moving laterally and trying to hide their tracks.

That is why every organization, regardless of who they are, even a political organization, must implement Cyber Attack Signals, and as part of its early warning system, implement unusual logs behavior. That will provide early warning and enable timely risk mitigation.

With a dashboard of Cyber Attack Signals, DNC (also the other two affiliated organizations) at the highest levels could have asked management these key questions:

- ❑ Are all the **Crown Jewels** in the scope of the Cyber Attack Signals?

- ❑ Are all privileged users who could be compromised to provide a quick path to the **Crown Jewels** identified for monitoring with Cyber Attack Signals?

- ❑ Does the Cyber Attack Signal, unusual logs behavior, cover all logs?

- ❑ What is the status of the investigation of anomalies detected in unusual logs behavior?

- ❑ What is the status of the investigation of anomalies detected in other Cyber Attack Signals?

Five key takeaways from this chapter

❏ The cyber attackers used a variety of tactics, techniques and procedures (TTPs) to hack into the Clinton campaign, DCCC and DNC network in order to steal more than 50,000 emails and documents, and worked with WikiLeaks to release the data during the U.S. presidential elections in an attempt to influence the elections.

❏ Had the Clinton campaign, DCCC and DNC implemented Cyber Attack Signals, the cyber attackers would most probably have been detected early and the data theft avoided. The cloud is not immune to a data breach. The email and documents stored on the premises and the analytics database in the cloud were equally susceptible and the attackers stole data from both using common TTPs. The Cyber Attack Signals were, therefore, necessary for monitoring both on the premises and in the cloud.

❏ The Cyber Attack Signals, abnormal logons and privileged users' behavior, would have most probably detected the widespread stealing of credentials and attempts to access the **Crown Jewels**. For example, the chairman of the Clinton campaign would have been identified as a privileged user and the signal, privileged users' behavior, would have monitored for anomalies and would have detected the attempted theft of the 50,000 emails from the chairman's account prior to exfiltration.

❏ The Cyber Attack Signal, **unusual logs behavior**, would most probably have detected the clearing and deletion of the logs by the attackers. The attackers made a lot of effort to clear and delete logs in order to hide, so the signal was key to timely detection.

❏ An event log captures and stores critical traffic, usage and behavior data about a network, users, system (such as Windows) or application. This data includes user logon sessions, account lockouts, failed password attempts, process start or end, application errors and closures. Cyber attackers will frequently either remove, stop, or clear event logs in order to prevent detection and destroy evidence of the cyber attack.

Chapter 10

Target: ICMP Packets

Chapter 10

Target: ICMP Packets

The Target data breach was one of the larger data breaches in history globally, with 110 million U.S. consumers' data being stolen by cyber attackers.

Here are the key highlights of the Target data breach.

- ❏ Target is a global retail chain and the second largest retailer in the U.S. with more than 1,700 store locations.

- ❏ Between November 12, 2013 and December 15, 2013, cyber attackers broke into Target's network, and stole credit-card and debit-card details and other personal and financial information of 110 million consumers.

Figure 1. Target timeline

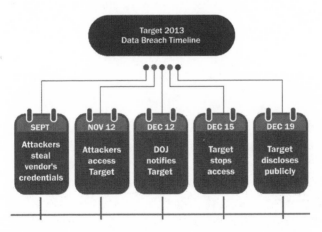

Figure 1 depicts the timeline of the Target data breach.[1]

The cyber attackers first gained access to Target's system by stealing credentials of a vendor, Fazio Mechanical Services, a refrigeration contractor with remote access to Target's network for electronic billing, contract submission and project management purposes. In September, two months before the Target data breach began, attackers stole Fazio's credentials for accessing Target's network via phishing emails infected with malware.

Using the stolen credentials, the cyber attackers broke into the Target network on November 12, 2013. For several days, the cyber attackers then performed internal reconnaissance and found a dump server that could be compromised with connectivity to Target's point-of-sale (POS) terminals. A POS terminal is a physical device used to process payments for goods the consumer purchases at a Target store.

They also found a file transfer protocol (FTP) server with outside connectivity that could be compromised for the data exfiltration.

Target's network was not properly segmented and the cyber attackers exploited this exposure to steal POS terminal administrator credentials and gain access to the POS terminals and consumers' payment and personal information.

The cyber attackers installed malware on a small number of POS terminals on November 15 to test it, and then installed the malware on the majority of Target's POS terminals and infected them by November 30. The cyber attackers then updated the malware. Target's malware intrusion detection system triggered alerts indicating potential suspicious activity but Target's security team did not react to the alerts.

As consumers swiped their cards at the POS terminals, the malware scraped the card number and other sensitive financial information from the memory and moved the data to the compromised dump server inside Target's network. The malware contained commands that mounted a drive on the dump server. The mapped network share was removed later to conceal the communications and the data transfer.

During the data transfer from the POS terminals to the dump server, the malware sent commands to send Internet Control Message Protocol (ICMP) packets from the POS terminals to the compromised FTP server to confirm once the data was scraped from the POS terminals and parked on the dump server.

Starting on December 2, 2013, the cyber attackers used the malware to start moving the data from the dump server to the FTP server and began the exfiltration of the data out of Target using encryption, and between the hours of 10 a.m. and 6 p.m., to blend in during normal business hours and with normal traffic.[2]

On December 12, 2013, the U.S. Department of Justice (DOJ) notified Target that consumer data was being advertised and sold on the black market relating to Target shoppers. Target then commenced an internal investigation. On December 15, 2013, it found and eliminated the cyber attackers' access and exfiltration.[3]

By this time, the cyber attackers had already completed exfiltration of more than 11 gigabytes of data.[4] On December 19, 2013, Target publicly disclosed the data breach involving theft of data impacting 40 million consumers.[5] On January 10, 2014, Target disclosed that a further 70 million consumers had been impacted.[6]

After the public disclosure, these events happened at Target:

- ❑ dozens of class-action lawsuits by consumer plaintiffs impacted from fraudulent transactions resulting from the data breach;
- ❑ class action lawsuits alleging the board of directors' breach of fiduciary duty and securities law violations;
- ❑ financial institutions' lawsuits involving those that issued the credit and debit cards that suffered losses from notifying impacted consumers, reissuing credit and debit cards, reimbursing consumers from fraudulent transactions, etc.;
- ❑ multiple federal and state regulatory agency and law enforcement investigations and lawsuits;
- ❑ congressional hearings and investigations;
- ❑ departure of Target's CEO, CISO and other management;
- ❑ negative impact to Target's stock price;
- ❑ reduction in sales and revenues and increase in expenses;
- ❑ negative publicity.

Signals missed

The cyber attackers initially broke in and gained a foothold on November 12, 2013. They remained undetected while moving around laterally and successfully getting to the **Crown Jewels** and stealing the data until December 15, 2013 when Target eliminated the attackers' access.

Here are the signals that were missed by Target in the critical steps of the Cyber Attack Chain:

❑ **lateral movement**
The cyber attackers were able to move laterally and were undetected for a period of more than a month. During that time, logon attempts using the stolen vendor users' credentials and other privileged users' credentials to logon to various Target systems provided signals. Reconnaissance to find the dump server and the FTP server and installation of malware on POS terminals also provided signals. Mounting the drive on the dump server and then removing the mapped network share once the data was moved also provided signals.

❑ **command and control**
ICMP packets from the POS terminals to the compromised FTP server to confirm once the data was scraped from the POS terminals and parked on the dump server provided critical signals. As cyber attackers firmed up the FTP server and communicated with it prior to beginning the data exfiltration, it provided signals.

Key takeaway lessons

Had Target implemented Cyber Attack Signals, the cyber attackers would most probably have been detected early and the data theft avoided.

❑ **lateral movement**
The Cyber Attack Signals, abnormal logons, privileged users' behavior, internal reconnaissance signals, malware signals and unusual logs behavior, would most probably have detected the cyber attackers' behavior multiple times and early on, starting with the

attackers using the vendor's stolen user credentials inside the Target network. The various Cyber Attack Signals would have provided Target multiple opportunities to detect the cyber attackers early.

❑ **command and control**
The Cyber Attack Signals, ICMP packets and C&C communications, would most probably have detected cyber attackers' behavior prior to exfiltration. ICMP packets would most probably have detected the unusual ICMP packets sent from the POS terminals to the compromised FTP server once the data was scraped from the POS terminals and parked on the dump server. As the FTP server was being firmed up for the upcoming exfiltration and the attackers communicated with the FTP server, C&C communications would most probably have detected this communication.

While Target's internal monitoring systems generated some alerts indicating unusual activity, and these alerts were not investigated, many signals were missed. The use of ICMP packets by the cyber attackers provided a major signal that was missed by Target. There was time and multiple opportunities to detect the unusual ICMP packets multiple times and prevent the exfiltration, because the malware sent commands to send ICMP packets from the POS terminals to the compromised FTP server to confirm each time the data was scraped from the POS terminals and parked on the dump server.

The size or the frequency and source and destination of ICMP packets going back and forth between servers and routers is a warning sign of a cyber theft about to happen, as was the case at Target, where the frequency and source and destination of the ICMP packets were abnormal. The ICMP packets generated from POS terminals and sent to the FTP server was abnormal, so was the frequency, since the ICMP packets were generated to confirm each batch of scraped data moved from the POS terminals to the dump server.

ICMP is a widely used method that uses packets containing messages, typically error or query messages, to enable servers and routers inside a network to communicate, for example, when a router is experiencing congestion or when a server is unreachable or unavailable. What was unusual in this case was ICMP packets going from POS terminals to the FTP server. Target did not detect this unusual activity involving the transmission of ICMP packets from the POS terminals to the FTP server.

The magnitude of the data breach at Target illustrates what can happen when critical signals are not monitored or are missed or are not acted upon promptly. That is why the senior management and board of directors at every organization must implement, as part of its early warning system, Cyber Attack Signals.

With a dashboard of Cyber Attack Signals, senior management and the board of directors at Target could have asked management these key questions:

- ❏ Are all **Crown Jewels** in the scope for monitoring with Cyber Attack Signals?

- ❏ Have all of the ways cyber attackers could get to the **Crown Jewels** in each Cyber Attack Chain step been identified?

- ❏ Have all relevant Cyber Attack Signals been identified to detect cyber attackers in each of the critical steps of the Cyber Attack Chain?

- ❏ Are the anomalies detected with the Cyber Attack Signals being investigated and what is the status of resolution?

- ❏ Does the Cyber Attack Signal, ICMP packets, not indicate anomalous behavior and what is the status of the investigation?

Five key takeaways from this chapter

❏ **ICMP** is a common method that uses packets containing messages, typically error or query messages, to enable servers and routers inside a network to communicate, for example, when a router is experiencing congestion or when a server is unreachable or unavailable.

❏ The size or the frequency and source and destination of ICMP packets going back and forth between servers and routers could, however, be a warning sign of a cyber theft about to happen, as was the case at Target, where the frequency and source and destination of the ICMP packets were abnormal.

❏ While Target's internal monitoring systems generated some alerts indicating unusual activity, and these alerts were not investigated, many signals were missed. Logon attempts using stolen vendor users' credentials and other privileged users' credentials to logon to various Target systems provided signals. Reconnaissance to find the dump server and the FTP server and installation of malware on POS terminals provided signals. Mounting the drive on the dump server and then removing the mapped network share once the data was moved also provided signals. As cyber attackers firmed up the FTP server and communicated with it prior to beginning the data exfiltration, it provided signals.

❏ The use of ICMP packets by the cyber attackers, however, provided a major signal that was missed by Target. The malware sent commands to send ICMP packets from the POS terminals to the compromised FTP server to confirm the data was scraped from the POS terminals and parked on the dump server.

❏ There was time and multiple opportunities to detect the unusual ICMP packets and prevent the exfiltration. The Cyber Attack Signal, **ICMP packets,** would most probably have detected and highlighted the unusual ICMP packets sent from the POS terminals to the compromised FTP server, each time the data was scraped from the POS terminals and parked on the dump server.

Chapter 11

SingHealth: C&C communications

Chapter 11

SingHealth: C&C communications

Singapore is a technology-savvy, city-country with a population of more than 5.6 million. It was the highest ranked city in the Global Smart City Performance Index, this ranking being based on Singapore's integration of Internet of Things (IoT) technologies and connected services.[1]

SingHealth is Singapore's largest healthcare organization. It consists of four public hospitals, including Singapore's largest hospital, Singapore General Hospital (SGH), five national specialty centers and nine polyclinics.

Even though SingHealth had various cybersecurity measures in place, cyber attackers broke into the network, evaded the defense, moved laterally undetected, and got to the **Crown Jewels**, SingHealth's Electronic Medical Records (EMR) database. They copied and successfully transmitted out personal information of 1.5 million patients and details of medical prescriptions of 160,000 patients, including the prime minister.[2,3] It was the largest data breach in Singapore's history.

The EMR database is part of the Sunrise Clinical Manager (SCM) software solution from Allscript Healthcare Solutions and is managed by Integrated Health Information System (IHiS), the central IT agency for the healthcare sector in Singapore.

The EMR database contains the following data for more than 5 million individual patients:

- ❏ patient demographic data;
- ❏ clinical episode information;
- ❏ doctor, nurse and clinician orders;
- ❏ medical exam and test results;
- ❏ clinical documentation;
- ❏ vital signs;
- ❏ medical alerts;

❏ allergies;
❏ diagnosis and health issues;
❏ vaccination details;
❏ discharge summaries;
❏ medical certificates;
❏ outpatient medication dispensed.

Figure 1. SingHealth timeline

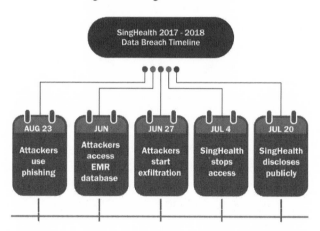

Figure 1 depicts the timeline of the SingHealth data breach.[4]

The cyber attackers used phishing emails to target SingHealth users and on August 23, 2017, one of the users fell victim. This particular user's workstation at SGH was running a Microsoft Outlook version that had not been patched for a vulnerability. The attackers were, therefore, able to exploit this unpatched vulnerability to gain a foothold. They were able to steal the user's credentials and insert customized malware to evade detection from SingHealth's antivirus software. The malware then called back to the cyber attackers' C&C server.

The attackers lay low for a while, and then moved laterally over the next several months between December 2017 and May 2018 to spread the malware to other workstations and steal the credentials of other users and administrators in the hunt for the **Crown Jewels**, the EMR database.

As they compromised other users' workstations, they used PowerShell to execute malicious commands and continue the lateral movement to the **Crown Jewels**.

Once the attackers found the EMR database, they made multiple attempts to log on to the database using the credentials they had stolen up to that point but these had insufficient privileges to gain access, so they repeatedly failed to get access to the EMR database.

From May to June 2018, the attackers used a compromised workstation and some Citrix local administrator accounts to log into Citrix servers in SGH, which eventually led to the EMR database. One of the administrator accounts had a password of P@ssw0rd, so it could easily be determined by the attackers. Also one of the servers, compromised by the attackers, with connectivity to the EMR database, had not been patched for more than a year for vulnerabilities.[5]

From June 27, 2018 to July 4, 2018, the attackers were able to run bulk queries on the EMR database to copy and transmit the data out. On July 4, 2018, the database administrators for IHiS detected the unusual bulk queries running on the EMR database, and took steps to shut down the attackers' access. It was, however, too late. The attackers had stolen data on 1.5 million patients.

Signals missed

The cyber attackers initially broke in and gained a foothold on August 23, 2017. By July 4, 2018, it was a period of more than 10 months that they had remained undetected while moving around laterally and successfully getting to the **Crown Jewels** and stealing the data. The following signals were missed by SingHealth in the critical steps of the Cyber Attack Chain:

❑ **intrusion**
SingHealth had not detected and escalated the unpatched work-station at SGH so it remained vulnerable. Beyond that, once the SGH user fell victim to the phishing attack on August 23, 2017, and as soon as the malware was installed, it communicated from

the user's workstation with the attackers C&C server, providing a signal. Additionally, the server with connectivity to the EMR database last received an update in May 2017, more than a year earlier, and this was also undetected and susceptible to exploitation by the attackers.

❑ **lateral movement**
The cyber attackers were able to move laterally undetected for more than 10 months. During that time, logon attempts using stolen user credentials to logon to other workstations, logon attempts with stolen privileged users' credentials and infection of malware to other workstations provided signals. PowerShell used to run malicious commands on workstations during the lateral movement was also a signal. Multiple attempted logons to the EMR database and failure to log on provided additional signals. Finally, after obtaining access to the EMR database, the bulk queries activated by stolen privileged users' credentials provided signals.

❑ **command and control**
The malware from the SGH user's workstation communicating with their C&C server upon intrusion in August 2017 was the initial signal, but several other times during the period of more than 10 months, as they moved laterally and infected other workstations with malware, signals were provided. Then as soon as they connected with their C&C server on June 27, 2018, and started to transmit out the data, a signal was provided.

Key takeaway lessons

Had SingHealth implemented Cyber Attack Signals, the cyber attackers would most probably have been detected early and the data theft avoided

❑ **intrusion**
The Cyber Attack Signal, patch window, would most probably have detected and escalated reporting of the unpatched SGH user workstation with the Microsoft Outlook vulnerability, and the un-

patched server with connectivity to the EMR database, which was not patched for more than a year.

❑ **lateral movement**

The Cyber Attack Signals, abnormal logons, privileged users' behavior, malicious PowerShell and malware signals, would most probably have detected cyber attackers' behavior multiple times and early on during a period of more than 10 months. The various signals would have provided SingHealth with multiple opportunities to detect the cyber attackers early.

Even when the cyber attackers got to the **Crown Jewels**, the EMR database, as it attempted to log on multiple times using the stolen credentials and failed multiple times, abnormal logons or privileged users' behavior, would most probably have provided timely detection of the cyber attack. As soon as the bulk queries were begun on the EMR database using a stolen privileged user's credentials, privileged users' behavior would most probably also have detected that.

❑ **command and control**

The Cyber Attack Signal, C&C communications, would most probably have detected the initial malware communication from the SGH user's workstation with the cyber attackers' C&C server in August 2017, and also at other times when the malware communicated with the C&C server from other infected workstations during the cyber attackers lateral movement during the 10 month plus period. On June 27, 2018, as soon the attackers communicated with their C&C server to begin the data transmission, C&C communications would most probably also have detected that and provided an opportunity to stop the data theft.

While there were several signals missed by SingHealth, C&C communications was a major signal missed in the intrusion, lateral movement and command and control steps in the Cyber Attack Chain.

Once malware is downloaded, unbeknownst to the victim, it is frequently designed to search for a way to communicate to a C&C server controlled by the cyber attackers. That communication provides confirmation to the cyber attackers that the malware has been activated and the entry point for the rest of the compromise has been attained.

From the initial entry point, the cyber attackers move laterally and hunt for other users and computers to infect with malware and compromise and extend the chain of compromised computers until the **Crown Jewels** are found.

The malware is frequently designed to communicate then with the C&C server either to start the exfiltration directly to the C&C server or to activate the exfiltration to a TOR dropper server (i.e. server on the TOR network that hides behind a proxy to keep the identity of the server anonymous). The TOR network is a service used to provide anonymity over the Internet and is used by governments and the public alike.

Figure 2. Typical flow

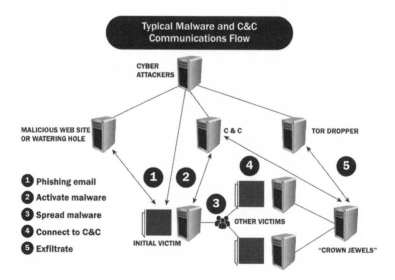

Figure 2 depicts a simple example of the typical flow with malware and C&C communications.

The C&C server and the communications with it enable the cyber attackers to perform crucial tasks to move laterally and exfiltrate the data or attain other objective. Without the C&C communications, the malware will not be able to operate fully and complete its mission in entirety.

While it is also important to look for some common signals of initial malware installation or early stage of propagation, because there are too many variants and because it will constantly change, the emphasis should be more on detecting signals of C&C communications in order to detect the malware, because C&C communications will be common to all malware.

Here are some common signals of C&C communications:

- ❏ requests to a numeric IP address as the domain name for the host;
- ❏ pattern of requests to certain IP addresses or hosts with frequency (i.e. hourly, daily or other frequency);
- ❏ multiple requests to hosts not ending with .com, .net or .org and host lengths greater than 30 characters;
- ❏ an abnormal number of DNS queries;
- ❏ multiple requests to dynamically generated algorithm (DGA) domains but with the same IP address;
- ❏ DNS query name domains not ending with .com, .net or .org and lengths greater than 30 characters;
- ❏ HTTPS communication using unauthorized SSL certificate with one-off name or unusual name or issued by unusual issuer;
- ❏ .dll file attempting to communicate with an unknown IP address;
- ❏ communication sessions with duration greater than 10 minutes;
- ❏ communication sessions involving download of data greater than 3 megabytes.

A key first step is to determine normal behavior patterns in terms of users, files, processes, tasks, sources and destinations, and network traffic and volumes. For example, for any server hosting shared network drive, anomalous activities should be identified for monitoring to signal attempted malware propagation. The network traffic baseline should also be determined (i.e. normal communication patterns, data volume, etc.) for different time windows (i.e. hourly, daily, etc.), devices and network services in order to identify anomalies.

An algorithm and tool with activity correlation capability will probably be necessary to automate the efficient and effective detection of anomalous behaviors indicating communications with the attackers' C&C server.

In SingHealth's case, once the SGH user fell victim to the phishing on August 23, 2017, and malware was installed, the malware communicated from the user's workstation with the attackers' C&C server. That was a major signal missed early on in the intrusion step.

Several other times during a period of more than 10 months, as the cyber attackers moved laterally and infected other workstations with malware and communicated with the C&C server, signals were missed in the lateral movement step.

The cyber attackers also ran queries and copied and transmitted out the data starting on June 27, 2018, until July 4, 2018. As soon as the attackers communicated with the C&C server to begin the transmission on June 27, the signal could have been detected in the command and control step, and the attack could have been shut down immediately, thus preventing the data theft.

The magnitude of the data breach at SingHealth illustrates what can happen when critical signals are not monitored for or are missed or are not acted upon promptly. While some of the IT staff did notice some suspicious activities, prior to detecting the queries on the EMR database on July 4, 2018, because there was no early-detection method in place as covered in this book, timely detection, proper reporting and prompt risk mitigation did not occur, and the cyber attackers remained in the network undetected over 10 months and stole the patients' data.[6]

That is why the senior management and board of directors at every organization must implement Cyber Attack Signals, and as part of its early warning system, implement C&C communications.

With a dashboard of Cyber Attack Signals, senior management and the board of directors at SingHealth could have asked management these key questions:

❏ Are all **Crown Jewels** in the scope for monitoring with Cyber Attack Signals?

❏ Have all of the ways cyber attackers could get to the **Crown Jewels** in each step of the Cyber Attack Chain been identified?

❏ Does the scope of the monitoring cover a comprehensive list of behaviors that may indicate C&C communications in each step of the Cyber Attack Chain?

❏ Does the monitoring use behavioral detection algorithms that are updated regularly for C&C communications behaviors?

❏ What is the status of investigations of anomalies indicated in C&C communications and with the other Cyber Attack Signals?

The SingHealth case touches our hearts. It involves the theft of patients' personal information, and details of medical prescriptions. Everyone is vulnerable, even the head of government.

All organizations have to take cybersecurity to the next level in order to do a better job to keep cyber attackers from stealing consumers' data. Consumers are counting on it.

Five key takeaways from this chapter

❑ Even though SingHealth had various cybersecurity measures in place, cyber attackers broke into the network, evaded the defense, moved laterally, and got to the **Crown Jewels**, the Electronic Medical Records (EMR) database. The attackers copied and transmitted out personal information of patients and details of medical prescriptions. This was the largest data breach in Singapore's history.

❑ The cyber attackers broke in and remained undetected for a period of more than 10 months while moving around laterally and successfully getting to the **Crown Jewels** and stealing the data. There were many signals, but the signals were not detected by SingHealth.

❑ The Cyber Attack Signal, **patch window**, would most probably have detected and escalated the reporting of the unpatched SGH user's workstation with the Microsoft Outlook vulnerability that provided the attackers the initial entry point. The patch window would most probably also have detected the unpatched server with connectivity to the EMR database, which was not patched for more than a year. The Cyber Attack Signals, abnormal logons, privileged users' behavior, malicious PowerShell and malware signals, would most probably also have provided multiple opportunities to detect the cyber attackers early.

❑ While there were several signals missed by SingHealth, C&C communications was a major signal missed in the intrusion, lateral movement and command and control steps in the Cyber Attack Chain. The Cyber Attack Signal, **C&C communications,** would most probably have detected the initial malware communication from the SGH user's workstation, and also at other times when the malware communicated with the C&C server from other infected workstations during the cyber attackers' lateral movement in the period of more than 10 months. As soon the attackers started to communicate with their C&C server to begin the data transmission, it would most probably have detected that and provided another opportunity to stop the data theft.

❑ The C&C server and the communications with it enable the cyber attackers to perform crucial tasks to move laterally and steal the data or inflict other harm. Without the C&C communications, any malware installed will not be able to operate fully. With malware, because there are too many variants and it will constantly change, the emphasis should be more on using the Cyber Attack Signal, **C&C communications**, to detect signals of communications with the C&C server in order to detect the malware, because C&C communications will be common to all malware. So the Cyber Attack Signal, C&C communications, is dual purpose; it detects early malware installation and propagation, but also C&C activities prior to data theft.

Chapter 12

Seven Steps to Detect Cyber Attackers Early

Chapter 12

Seven Steps to Detect Cyber Attackers Early

Having looked in detail at seven significant cybersecurity cases, you will have seen in each of these cases that the Cyber Attack Signals were there but were not detected. Had these organizations detected the signals, the cyber attackers would most probably have been thwarted and the damage avoided. You should now begin to have a better understanding of why implementing Cyber Attack Signals is the game changer.

It is only a matter of time before the cyber attackers will intrude, so the key to success is early detection of the signals of the cyber attackers at work, prior to the execution of the cyber attack. Detecting signals of the cyber attackers is of greatest value before the cyber attack is executed in the Cyber Attack Chain (i.e. detection in the intrusion, lateral movement and command and control steps).

Many organizations or their technology providers that support them have supplemented their intrusion prevention system (IPS) or intrusion detection system (IDS) with a security information and event management (SIEM) system to detect the cyber attackers.

These SIEMs ingest vast amounts of data from the IPS or IDS and a variety of logs and data on network traffic volume. Then they normalize and analyze the data, correlate and then aggregate and report signals of possible cyber attack activity.

No doubt, a SIEM is a critical detection technology tool that is necessary in the fight. The problem, however, is that the SIEMs kick out a large number of alerts, and a large number of those alerts are false positives (i.e. false indicators of cyber attackers). Each year, there are increasing levels of uninvestigated SIEM alerts across the globe. Alert fatigue (i.e. too many alerts, not enough resources, inability to discern signal from noise and high levels of false positives) are causing high rates of uninvestigated alerts.

Additionally, frequently the SIEM's scope is not properly configured and calibrated to map to the **Crown Jewels**, so it fails to generate alerts of cyber attack activity targeting the **Crown Jewels**. Data science and artificial intelligence (AI) are being added to the mix, with additional investment, in order to improve the accuracy of the alerts and reduce false positives, but there is still a long way to travel.

Simply rushing to buy a SIEM or buying a more expensive SIEM with data science or AI capability is, therefore, not the answer to detecting the cyber attackers in the Cyber Attack Chain in a timely manner. What then is the answer?

The answer instead is to implement the game changer; to put into operation the system of Cyber Attack Signals in these seven methodical steps.

 Identify all Crown Jewels.

We must begin with the end in mind, namely the **Crown Jewels**. After all, it is the ultimate target of the cyber attackers. The cyber attackers are after the **Crown Jewels**, so it is important to recognize that and start there. The cyber attackers goal is to infiltrate the network (whether on the premises or in the cloud) and find the **Crown Jewels**, and then to steal it or hijack it and disrupt operations and cause financial or other damage. So the first step towards success is to identify *all* of the **Crown Jewels** of the organization.

Crown Jewels are all of the mission critical and sensitive data, including consumer data, intellectual property and technology assets of the organization.

So the first step is to prepare a comprehensive inventory of *all* of the **Crown Jewels** of the organization. Here are examples of what should be identified as **Crown Jewels**:

❑ databases containing consumer non-public personally identifiable information (NPI), personal health information (PHI), credit-card details, financial information or other sensitive information;

- ❑ databases containing the organization's intellectual property, such as product designs, patents, business plans, technology architecture, network cybersecurity designs, financial information and research and development data;
- ❑ databases containing customer lists, customer contracts, supplier contracts, sales reports, employee payroll information, etc.;
- ❑ databases containing privileged users' credential information;
- ❑ databases containing users' credential information;
- ❑ Internet of Things (IoT) devices or servers containing NPI, PHI or intellectual property or with connectivity to the **Crown Jewels**;
- ❑ servers hosting email, files, databases, logs or backups;
- ❑ servers storing archives of databases or backups;
- ❑ servers used for software development, testing and updates;
- ❑ computers used by privileged users;
- ❑ computers used by contractors or suppliers to access the network via VPN.

The scope of the inventory must be comprehensive and accurate so as not to miss an asset that the cyber attackers could target and must include assets beyond just databases, such as servers and computers containing valuable data or providing valuable capabilities to the cyber attackers. Optimally, in addition to the inventory, a visual diagram of all of the **Crown Jewels** depicted inside the network and any interconnectivity should be documented.

The first step must be to identify adequately *all* **Crown Jewels** to get a complete picture of what the most critical assets are and what the attack surface is that the cyber attackers will have available to target. Fully understanding what the **Crown Jewels** are and where they are located is a significant challenge facing organizations globally, especially larger organizations. The organization must devote adequate resources to get this right at the beginning, otherwise it will always be one step behind the cyber attackers and will always have blind spots. Internet of Things (IoT) devices (commonly referred to as Industrial Internet of Things (IIoT) devices by industrial companies) must not be missed when determining what the **Crown Jewels** are. IoT devices (sometimes referred to as smart devices) communicate with the Internet to send or receive data.

IoT devices targeted by cyber attackers include routers, IoT servers, wireless radio links, smart TVs, audio/video streaming devices, IP cameras, DVRs, smart printers or scanners, satellite antenna equipment, controllers, smart temperature, heat, smoke or chemical sensors, mobile devices, kiosks, heart pacemaker monitors, smart garage door openers and network-attached storage devices.

IoT devices create opportunities for cyber attackers to inflict safety hazards. For example, the U.S. Food and Drug Administration (FDA) alerted consumers to a recall of 465,000 heart pacemakers, noting security vulnerabilities in the IoT devices that could allow cyber attackers to drain the pacemaker's battery rapidly or to adjust the operation of the device.[1]

In another case, cyber attackers used the Mirai botnet, composed of IoT devices, such as IP cameras and routers, infected with malicious software, to execute a distributed denial of service (DDoS) attack worldwide. The breadth of the attack was massive, impacting all types of organizations.

One of the victims was a residential building management system in Finland. The attackers blocked Internet access, sending the connected management system into an endless cycle of rebooting. This left the apartment residents with no central heating in the middle of winter for a week.[2]

In another example, researchers discovered vulnerabilities in Internet-connected gas-station pumps. With remote access, the attackers could not only steal credit-card information but also change the temperature and pressure in the gas tanks, potentially causing explosions.[3]

Organizations of all types in a variety of sectors are increasingly deploying IoT devices and supporting assets such as IoT servers. These devices are highly susceptible to a cyber attack. An organization must take care to identify *all* IoT devices and supporting assets and whether they provide a gateway to the **Crown Jewels** or whether they should be classified as **Crown Jewels** on their own because the devices or supporting assets contain NPI, PHI or intellectual property and will most probably be a target for cyber attackers.

IoT devices are inherently high risk because frequently manufacturers of these devices are slow to release patches for vulnerabilities or may not be around to keep the device updated, or often they manufacture them without adequate security at the forefront or with preconfigured passwords which are not changed prior to deployment. Untimely patching of a vulnerability or unchanged default passwords are two examples of exposures with IoT devices that cyber attackers exploit.

Many cities are using IoT technology innovatively to deliver services, but at the same time are vulnerable to cyber attackers because of security weaknesses. IBM X-Force Red and Threatcare revealed the following features in the *Dangers of Smart City Hacking* Ethical Hacking Whitepaper.[4]

- ❑ 17 zero-day vulnerabilities were identified in smart-city sensor and control devices deployed across the globe by various municipalities.

- ❑ Those vulnerabilities included:
  - o **weak password security**
    The devices could be placed into operations without requiring the user to create a secure password or the user could create weak passwords, such as "admin".

  - o **weak authentication controls allowing bypass**
    The login could be bypassed and the administrator menu page that normally only an internal administrator should have to access to could be called up.

  - o **SQL injection vulnerability**
    SQL injection could be inserted and used for further exploitation.

- ❑ Every device examined was still using the default passwords that came with the device, which are easily found online. In addition, all of the devices had authentication bypass issues.

In the case of industrial and utilities companies, unfortunately, many organizations have not yet adequately focused on the risks inherent in IoT devices and supporting assets and detection of cyber attackers.

For example, according to the IBM Institute for Business Value Benchmarking Study of 700 industrial and utilities company executives, the respondents surveyed said while implementing IoT that only 25 percent had implemented IoT threat detection and only 10 percent had implemented continuous monitoring of IoT traffic to find anomalies and assess vulnerabilities.[5]

So a lot of work lies ahead for many organizations in a variety of sectors who are deploying IoT and are inherently high risk.

2 **Identify high probability TTPs for each Crown Jewel.**

Regardless of the type of organization, once *all* of the **Crown Jewels** are identified, the next step is to take each **Crown Jewel** and identify high-probability scenarios involving cyber attackers, using tactics, techniques and procedures (TTPs) in the Cyber Attack Chain to steal the **Crown Jewels** or hijack it and cause disruption and financial or other damage.

The Adversarial Tactics, Techniques and Common Knowledge (AT-T&CK) for Enterprise is developed by MITRE.[6] It is an authoritative model that describes the TTPs that cyber attackers will tend to take to infiltrate, perform lateral movement and execute data exfiltration or other objective in each of the steps of the MITRE-defined Cyber Attack Lifecycle model.

One item to note is that MITRE's Cyber Attack Lifecycle model depicts exfiltration as the step before command and control, whereas my Cyber Attack Chain model depicts execution as the final step after command and control.

The Cyber Attack Chain model's logic is that execution is the final step in the cyber attack and all other steps, including command and control activities are necessary before being able to execute (i.e. exfiltrate data or attain other objective).

Regardless of this difference between the two models, MITRE's ATT&CK is a constantly growing common reference and a body of knowledge for cyber attackers' behavior. It is a valuable resource for an organization to use as a starting point and as a baseline. The organization should add to the model other TTPs it may be aware of or identify as relevant for its **Crown Jewels**.

Another valuable resource to consult is the OWASP Top 10 listing the most impactful application security risks currently facing organizations.[7] There is also the OWASP Top Internet of Things (IoT) Vulnerabilities listing the major IoT vulnerabilities and the associated attack surfaces.[8]

The key is to think of highly probable scenarios involving TTPs that cyber attackers could use to get to the **Crown Jewels** and steal data or to attain other objective, such as use ransomware to disrupt operations and inflict financial and other damages. The TTPs in MITRE's ATT&CK model provides a good starting point.

 Map Cyber Attack Signals for each Crown Jewel.

The next step is to identify the Cyber Attack Signals relevant at each step in the Cyber Attack Chain that would most probably detect cyber attackers' behavior and activity as they try to get to each **Crown Jewel**. By doing that, relevant Cyber Attack Signals are identified methodically for each **Crown Jewel** and no asset is missed that the cyber attackers could target.

The key is to map relevant Cyber Attack Signals in each step in the Cyber Attack Chain that would most probably detect cyber attackers as they use TTPs to get to each **Crown Jewel**. Mapping relevant Cyber Attack Signals in each step for each Crown Jewel ensures multiple opportunities to detect cyber attackers, so that if for some reason a signal of the cyber attackers is missed in a particular step, another signal can detect the attackers in another step.

In addition to the Top 15 Cyber Attack Signals identified in this book, MI-TRE's Cyber Analytics Repository (CAR) contains a list of behavioral analytics and is another valuable resource to consult when identifying relevant cyber attack signals.[9]

Figure 1 and 2 illustrate two examples of a **Crown Jewels analysis** and how each **Crown Jewel** could be mapped to TTPs and Cyber Attack Signals in critical steps of the Cyber Attack Chain in order to detect cyber attackers' activity and behavior in a timely manner, and prevent the theft of the assets or hijacking of the assets and disruption of operations causing financial or other damage. The source for the TTPs in Figure 1 and 2 is MITRE's ATT&CK model.

Figure 1. **Crown Jewel # 1**

Crown Jewel# 1 Cyber Attack Signals					
Crown Jewel # 1					
			Cyber Attack Chain		
TTPs	External Reconnaissance	Intrusion	Lateral Movement	Command & Control	Execution
Exploit Public Facing Application		Patch Window			
Command Line Interface		Web Shell			
Logon Scripts			Abnormal Logons		
Exploitation for Privileged Access			Privileged Users' Behavior		
Windows Remote Management			Malware Signals		
File Deletion			Unusual Logs Behavior		
Custom Command & Control Protocol				C&C Communications	

Figure 1 relates to **Crown Jewel # 1,** a database that stores hundreds of consumer complaints information from the website forms filled out by consumers, including social security number, driver's license number, date of birth, name, address, email and phone number and details of financial information related to the complaint, such as credit-card numbers. Breaking into the network and stealing this data would provide the cyber attackers with an extremely valuable asset.

Figure 1 illustrates a simple but effective method to capture high probability TTPs that the cyber attackers could use during the critical steps of the Cyber Attack Chain to break in, perform lateral movement, and exfiltrate the data and the countermeasure Cyber Attack Signals that would most probably provide the signals to detect the cyber attackers prior to exfiltration of the data.

Figure 2. **Crown Jewel** # 2

Crown Jewel # 2					
			Cyber Attack Chain		
TTPs	External Reconnaissance	Intrusion	Lateral Movement	Command & Control	Execution
File Systems Permission Weakness		Patch Window			
Exploitation for Privileged Access			Privileged Users' Behavior		
Exploitation for Defense Evasion			Malicious PowerShell		
Custom Cryptographic Protocol			Ransomware Signals		
Remote Desktop Protocol			RDP Signals		
File Deletion			Unusual Logs Behavior		
Custom Command & Control Protocol				C&C Communications	

Figure 2 relates to **Crown Jewel # 2,** a database that stores hundreds of critical, highly confidential intellectual-property documents necessary to run daily operations. Without access to this database, daily operations will be disrupted and financial damages will be incurred. Installing ransomware to block access to this critical database would disrupt operations and cause financial damage and provide the cyber attackers the opportunity to demand a hefty ransom.

Figure 2 illustrates a simple but effective method to capture high-probability TTPs that the cyber attackers could use during the critical steps of the Cyber Attack Chain to break in, perform lateral movement, and install the ransomware and the countermeasure Cyber Attack Signals that would most probably provide the signals to detect the cyber attackers prior to full installation of the ransomware and disruption of operations.

The key is to identify *all* **Crown Jewels** and then to identify for each high-probability scenarios involving the cyber attackers using TTPs in the Cyber Attack Chain and map relevant Cyber Attack Signals in each step that would most probably detect cyber attackers' activity and behavior for each **Crown Jewel**, as illustrated in Figure 1 and 2.

While the two examples in Figure 1 and 2 focus on mapping relevant Cyber Attack Signals in the intrusion, lateral movement and command and control steps in the Cyber Attack Chain, an organization could also map relevant Cyber Attack Signals in the external reconnaissance and execution steps if it desired to do so. Additional TTPs at each step could also be identified if relevant for the particular **Crown Jewel**.

A key point to note is that in some instances it may make sense to map multiple Cyber Attack Signals to detect a TTP for a **Crown Jewel**. Also, once the Cyber Attack Signals are mapped for each **Crown Jewel**, it will become evident which Cyber Attack Signals could be aggregated to detect signals of the cyber attackers with efficiency. In some instances, it will make sense to aggregate and generate a Cyber Attack Signal applicable to multiple **Crown Jewels**, while in other instances, it will be necessary to generate a Cyber Attack Signal specific to a **Crown Jewel**, given its unique nature.

Additionally, as you'll notice in both Figure 1 and 2, the Cyber Attack Signal, patch window, was identified as relevant for both **Crown Jewels**. The patch window should always be identified as a relevant Cyber Attack Signal for each **Crown Jewel** as a matter of practice, regardless of what the **Crown Jewel** is or what relevant scenarios or TTPs are identified for the **Crown Jewel** or whether a vulnerability has been reported at that point in time applicable to a **Crown Jewel**.

This discipline will make sure no unmitigated vulnerabilities relevant to a **Crown Jewel** is missed and is the root cause for cyber attackers slipping into the network, remaining undetected and stealing the data or inflicting other harm.

Figure 3. **Crown Jewels** analysis

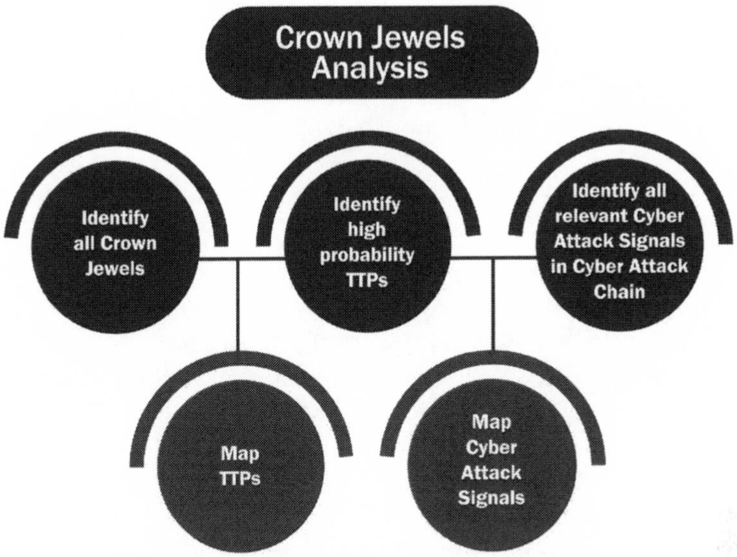

Figure 3 summarizes the overall **Crown Jewels** analysis approach.

In summary, **Crown Jewels** analysis, comprised of Steps 1-3 of the overall seven-step method ensures the focus is on the **Crown Jewels**, just like it is for the cyber attackers, and that no **Crown Jewels** are missed and the focus is on TTPs most probably to be deployed by the cyber attackers so that relevant signals for each **Crown Jewel** is monitored for and so that the monitoring and detection is effective and delivers results on time.

Unfortunately, this is not what is happening today. Today, in many instances, the monitoring is not covering *all* **Crown Jewels**. High-risk IoT devices and servers are being missed in the scope and a lot of noise is being generated from the monitoring, and organizations are struggling to determine what is a signal versus a false positive while the cyber attackers are successfully avoiding detection, finding the **Crown Jewels** and stealing the data or inflicting other harm.

4 **Generate Cyber Attack Signals.·**

Once the **Crown Jewels** analysis is completed and relevant Cyber Attack Signals are identified for each **Crown Jewel**, the next step is to identify all data sources and leverage the SIEM or another tool in order to generate the Cyber Attack Signals to detect cyber attackers early in the Cyber Attack Chain.

For the Cyber Attack Signal, patch window, which will need to be identified for each **Crown Jewel**, the source will need to be MITRE's Common Vulnerabilities and Exposures (CVE) list of publicly known cybersecurity vulnerabilities with Common Vulnerability Scoring System (CVSS) risk scores. MITRE provides CVSS scores for almost all known vulnerabilities. The CVE with the CVSS score for a publicly announced vulnerability will help generate the Cyber Attack Signal, patch window, for each **Crown Jewel**.

Additionally, any internally or externally conducted vulnerability scan results, penetration test results or outside security researcher detected vulnerabilities, should be added as a source for the Cyber Attack Signal, patch window.

Not always will there be applicable CVEs or scan results relating to a **Crown Jewel** since there may be no CVEs or unpatched vulnerability relating to a **Crown Jewel** at that point in time, but the discipline of generating the Cyber Attack Signal, patch window, will ensure no **Crown Jewel** with an unpatched vulnerability is missed.

For the other relevant Cyber Attack Signals for each **Crown Jewel**, the SIEM and other sources will need to be used in order to generate the Cyber Attack Signals.

For example, some organizations may still be analyzing the logs directly instead of feeding them into a SIEM and using the SIEM's analytics or using open-source SIEM-type tools and not have invested in a commercial SIEM or a sophisticated SIEM with data science or AI capability as of now, due to the high cost of the SIEM.

Regardless, even for organizations with a SIEM in place, additional logs that may not yet be fed to the SIEM, such as endpoint logs, should be included in the scope to boost the quality and effectiveness of the Cyber Attack Signals. Endpoint logs can be operationalized to provide deeper signals of cyber attackers' activity, such as on desktops/laptops, and increase the depth and breadth of the source of the Cyber Attack Signals.

Once all data sources that are necessary are identified and verified in order to be able to generate the Cyber Attack Signals, if the organization or its technology provider utilizes a SIEM, then the SIEM could be leveraged as the central repository for all data sources for the Cyber Attack Signals for each **Crown Jewel**.

The additional data sources, such as the CVE and CVSS data, could be fed into the SIEM to supplement the data that is already going into the SIEM to generate the Cyber Attack Signals. This way the existing SIEM and its analytical capabilities are taken advantage of instead of recreating the wheel.

If the organization or its technology provider that utilizes either a commercial SIEM or an open-source SIEM type tool cannot configure it for some reason, it will need to utilize another tool to generate the Cyber Attack Signals. That will also be the case for an organization that as of now is not using a SIEM or an open-source SIEM-type tool.

Figure 4. Leveraging existing SIEM

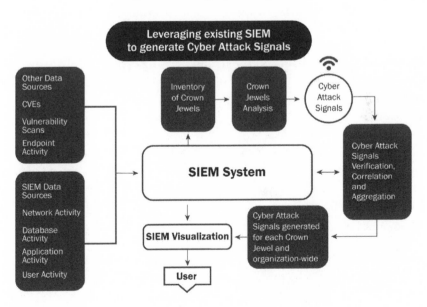

155

Figure 4 shows an example of how an existing SIEM could be leveraged to generate the Cyber Attack Signals.

Figure 4 illustrates how the SIEM could be configured to generate Cyber Attack Signals for each **Crown Jewel.** The flow chart shows how additional data sources, such as CVEs, vulnerability scans, code reviews and endpoint activity, can be added to the data sources typically feeding the SIEM, such as network, database, application or user activity.

Also, how the existing SIEM and its analytical capabilities can be taken advantage of to generate Cyber Attack Signals for each **Crown Jewel**, and also in aggregate for the entire organization, to detect signals of the cyber attackers.

The existing SIEM's visualization capabilities can also potentially be leveraged via its dashboard, reports and email-notification features.

The cyber attack signals and SIEM alerts are in essence analogous to key risk indicators (KRIs) and risk indicators or key performance indicators (KPIs) and performance indicators respectively. In other words, the Cyber Attack Signals are the key alerts, focusing on each **Crown Jewel** with signals of high-probability cyber attack activity (because it focuses on behavior) in the Cyber Attack Chain, compared to all of the alerts generated from the SIEM.

Generating the Cyber Attack Signals and tracking their value also provides the opportunity to fine-tune and cull the SIEM alerts to reduce false positives and all of the noise by focusing on the **Crown Jewels** and generating signals that provide maximum value.

Currently, a SIEM will also probably be fed threat intelligence (i.e. intelligence on current cyber attacks) and indicators of compromise (IOCs), which are forensically discovered evidence of cyber attackers' activity from other cyber attacks, so that it can analyze and search for and trigger alerts of any signs of similar IOCs at the organization.

The challenge, however, is that the IOCs that the SIEM is being fed are primarily reactive, and the alerts that it is generating after analysis and searching for are specific or granular, such as a specific IP address or email address, or calculated or derived, such as the hash of a detected malicious file or malware.

In most cases, the IOCs are not proactive and behavioral (i.e. focused proactively on signals of TTPs and cyber attackers' behavior) and also are not mapped to each **Crown Jewel**. This is a key reason why there are a lot of false positives and a lot of noise being generated currently while the cyber attackers are able to dodge and weave and slip by and get to the **Crown Jewels** undetected.

Implementing the system of Cyber Attack Signals enables mapping to and focusing on each **Crown Jewel** so none are missed and on detecting cyber attackers' behavior while trying to get to the **Crown Jewels**.

Cyber Attack Signals are not just based on forensic evidence from the latest compromise or malware, but instead are derived from cyber attackers' behavior based on commonality of TTPs used and detects signals of cyber attackers' behavior in each step in the Cyber Attack Chain, relevant for each **Crown Jewel**.

Each organization should develop a list of Cyber Attack Signals for each **Crown Jewel** and in aggregate. Those signals are resilient because they are independent of specific tools, malware or ransomware that may be used, which can be changed very quickly by the cyber attackers, and instead detect the cyber attackers by focusing on common behaviors that are most probably to be performed in each step of the Cyber Attack Chain.

MITRE's Technical Report *Finding Cyber Threat with ATT&CK-Based Analytics* identified that cyber attackers exhibit consistent patterns of behavior post-intrusion, and results of MITRE's research indicated that focusing on signals of cyber attackers' behavior post-intrusion using analytics was a practical way to separate all of the noise generated from normal system use to detect the cyber attackers. MITRE also validated its research findings on both the behavioral analytics and the efficacy of using the analytics to detect the cyber attackers through a series of cyber games.[10]

Leveraging the SIEM as the central repository for all data sources for Cyber Attack Signals and utilizing it to generate Cyber Attack Signals focused on cyber attackers' behavior will provide actionable intelligence not only focused on the **Crown Jewels** but will also lead to detecting cyber attackers' activity early, while deriving greater value from the SIEM.

In that way, the SIEM will be refined over time to generate fewer alerts that will be more accurate, prioritized, meaningful and timely.

If the organization or its technology provider does not utilize a SIEM or cannot configure the SIEM to leverage it to generate the Cyber Attack Signals for some reason, it will of course need to utilize another tool to generate the Cyber Attack Signals. It is an ideal use case for an AI tool.

Regardless of whether the organization utilizes, partially a cloud provider (such as the Big Six, comprised of Amazon Web Services (AWS), Microsoft Azure, Google Cloud, Rackspace, Oracle Cloud and IBM Cloud) for some infrastructure or services, or whether it has completely outsourced its infrastructure or services to a cloud provider, it will need to recognize that ultimately it owns cybersecurity and that it is responsible for security *in* the cloud, whereas the cloud provider is responsible for security *of* the cloud.

While the cloud provider will provide the perimeter security, the organization is responsible for security of its data and IP and other assets that are in the cloud (i.e. its **Crown Jewels**).

So organizations are equally susceptible to cyber attackers in the cloud. Even with the sophisticated cloud providers, such as the Big Six, providing cybersecurity, cyber attackers can still exploit the weaker links in the chain and break in and steal the data or inflict other harm. For example, simply stealing credentials of a privileged user will provide the 'keys to the kingdom' regardless of how strong the security is from the cloud provider.

Consider the Uber case. Cyber attackers gained access to Uber's private GitHub repository, a coding site used by Uber software developers, where they discovered the AWS account credentials. The attackers then used these credentials to log into Uber's AWS account undetected. There they found the archive of rider and driver information, which they download-ed undetected. This download included data on 57 million customers and drivers, including names, email addresses, phone numbers and driver's li-cense numbers.[11]

Also, a growing trend is not stealing data from the cloud but instead steal-ing the compute power of the cloud to do cryptomining (i.e. mining Bit-coin) under the radar, without the knowledge of the cloud provider or the organization, also referred to as cryptojacking.

Look at the Aviva case. Aviva is a U.K. insurance company with 33 million customers. Cyber attackers identified that Aviva's administration console was deployed on an AWS cloud without a username and password and the AWS access keys and secret tokens were visible. The attackers exploited this security gap and stole the credentials to activate a MySQL12 container in AWS to execute Bitcoin mining commands, undetected by Aviva, until RedLock brought this to Aviva's attention and the exploit was then shut down.[12]

So the cloud environment presents an additional twist, the risk of not only the theft of data, but also theft of compute power by the cyber attackers without detection. As the organization identifies its **Crown Jewels** in a cloud environment, it will, therefore, need to consider the assets that can be hijacked for compute power, because cyber attackers will target these assets in the cloud.

Regardless, in a cloud environment, the organization will still need to de-termine the critical Cyber Attack Signals it will need to focus monitoring on, based on the **Crown Jewels** analysis and its risk profile.

Some of the Cyber Attack Signals will be the same whether in a cloud envi-ronment or on the premises (e.g. abnormal logons, privileged users' behav-ior or unusual logs behavior), and others will be even more relevant and heightened for a cloud environment (e.g. C&C communications) to detect anomalous application programming interface (API) communications from or to a C&C server. API communications will be prevalent in a cloud environment, so the need to detect anomalous activity will be heightened.

It will also be more likely that the cloud provider will provide an out-of-the box monitoring service with a dashboard, but the organization will need to configure or customize this monitoring to make sure the end outcome is a dashboard of Cyber Attack Signals that are mapped to the **Crown Jewels** after a **Crown Jewels** analysis is completed, as covered in this book.

A big mistake will be simply to start using the out-of-the box monitoring service and dashboard without the **Crown Jewels** analysis and mapping to Cyber Attack Signals and configuring or customizing the monitoring service and dashboard to generate the Cyber Attack Signals. Otherwise, the out-of-box monitoring service and dashboard will generate false positive signals, untimely signals or no signals at all from missed **Crown Jewels**.

Consider the Capital One case. The data for 106 million consumers and small businesses was stolen from the cloud. A web application firewall misconfiguration allowed the attacker to break in. Lack of monitoring of Cyber Attack Signals (such as privileged users' behavior), mapped to the credit card applications data repository, allowed the attacker to exfiltrate the data undetected.

Whether on the premises or in the cloud, the key to success is to make sure the Cyber Attack Signals are mapped to the **Crown Jewels** and focus on detecting cyber attackers' behavior early in the Cyber Attack Chain.

5 Supplement Cyber Attack Signals.

In addition to generating Cyber Attack Signals for each **Crown Jewel**, what is also necessary is to implement honeypots and threat hunting to supplement the system of Cyber Attack Signals in order to increase the chances of detecting the cyber attackers in a timely manner.

Honeypots broadly are assets (servers, laptops, databases, fake user credentials, etc.) that are inserted into the production environment in order to lure and fake the cyber attackers. They mimic what is on the production environment but are set up so they are not used by anyone in the organization.

The value of honeypots is to increase the chances of detecting the cyber attackers, since any access to the honeypot will signal cyber attackers as no one else in the organization should be accessing the honeypot.

Utilizing honeypots requires proper planning and execution in order to avoid providing access inadvertently to normal users in the organization or to avoid suspicion by the cyber attackers that they have stumbled into a honeypot.

While honeypots have currently been adopted by some organizations, all organizations need to consider adopting honeypots in addition to a system of Cyber Attack Signals in order to transform the defense into offense. The honeypot could be included as part of the scope of the **Crown Jewels** and subjected to a **Crown Jewels** analysis and the implementation of applicable Cyber Attack Signals. If cyber attackers were to access any part of the honeypot, it would definitely detect the cyber attackers' activity so that prompt action could be taken to remove the cyber attackers and prevent any damage to the actual **Crown Jewels**.

In addition to honeypots, threat hunting should also be implemented. Threat hunting is essentially a human process to supplement the automated process to search the network proactively to detect cyber attackers' activity. In that way, there are increased chances of detecting the cyber attackers in a timely manner without relying completely on automated detection. A key value of threat hunting is improving the automated detection by identifying new TTPs and feeding the system new signals to look for.

A team of threat hunters could be assigned the task to focus on the **Crown Jewels** and to investigate promptly the signals of cyber attackers' activity generated from the system of Cyber Attack Signals and take prompt action to prevent damage to the **Crown Jewels**.

With this process, the team will inevitably learn new TTPs or identify new TTPs similar to what the cyber attackers were perpetrating and could provide this feedback to modify or create new Cyber Attack Signals to automate using the SIEM or another tool. The team of threat hunters can also recommend supplementing the mapped Cyber Attack Signals with new signals based on new and emerging threats relevant to the **Crown Jewels**.

What is also critical to success is transforming the employees in the organization into threat scouts. While organizations today provide security-awareness training to employees, the training is rudimentary and does not teach signals of cyber attackers to look out for in the day-to-day operations so that every person in the organization can become an early-warning system.

The training needs to go beyond warnings against falling victim to phishing (malicious emails) or vishing (social engineering phone calls) and instead use gaming techniques to simulate real world TTPs that cyber attackers use in each step of the Cyber Attack Chain to get to the **Crown Jewels**, and the signals to detect, in a fun, engaging way to make the training highly effective and convert each person into a threat scout and supplement the automated detection via the Cyber Attack Signals.

 Update Crown Jewels analysis for significant changes, threats and risk factors.

Additionally, the **Crown Jewels** analysis involving high-probability scenarios of cyber attackers using TTPs and mapping to relevant Cyber Attack Signals will need to be updated periodically to reflect new, high-probability threats or reflect significant changes that occur in the organization impacting the **Crown Jewels**.

The following are some examples of drivers triggering an updated **Crown Jewels** analysis:

❑ an acquisition or a merger with another organization leading to the addition of new **Crown Jewels** or expansion of existing **Crown Jewels**;

❑ a new supplier or a new partner added with access to the network or access to any assets that could be connected to the **Crown Jewels**;

- ❑ new technologies or databases introduced to the network on the premises or in the cloud;
- ❑ new Internet of Things (IoT) devices or supporting IoT servers connected to the network on the premises or in the cloud;
- ❑ new **Crown Jewels** created or added to the organization;
- ❑ new product or service launches impacting the **Crown Jewels;**
- ❑ new VPN access added to the network on the premises or in the cloud;
- ❑ expansion geographically of facilities, offices and staffing;
- ❑ new hiring or firing or layoffs of privileged users;
- ❑ significant changes in suppliers or partners with access to the network or access to any assets that could be connected to the **Crown Jewels,** such as acquisition or merger or new hiring or firing or layoffs of privileged users or significant changes to its network or cybersecurity or significant changes downstream in the suppliers' or partners' chains.

The mapping of Cyber Attack Signals to monitor each **Crown Jewel** is the beginning and not the end of the game-winning strategy, and is a dynamic and not a one-time exercise in order to stay one step ahead of the cyber attackers. As such, the **Crown Jewels** analysis must be updated periodically to incorporate significant changes, threats or risk factors such as those identified in these examples.

 Provide dashboard of Cyber Attack Signals to the highest levels regularly.

Finally, the Cyber Attack Signals generated for each **Crown Jewel** and the results of the monitoring for each **Crown Jewel** and in aggregate for the entire organization must be tracked and reported in a dashboard to the highest levels (i.e. senior management and board of directors) regularly and promptly.

This reporting will facilitate proper and timely oversight from the highest levels. Cybersecurity cannot be a back-office IT issue; instead it must be front and center and a boardroom issue and a priority. Cyber risk is one of the most significant and disruptive risks faced by almost every organization and protecting the **Crown Jewels** must be the top priority at the highest levels.

Think about the time that is being spent on and what is being reviewed on strategy, financials and operations in your organization today with senior management and the board. Then think about how much time is being spent on and what is being reviewed on cybersecurity today. Are they equal in time and quality?

Unfortunately, today in most organizations, either cybersecurity is given very little time or time is wasted away reviewing information or metrics that provide false comfort. The information being presented and reviewed on cybersecurity is from the lens of "Here is what we are spending money on and here is what we are doing to prevent the hack and here are metrics that show we have prevented a hack."

The information on cybersecurity must be presented and reviewed from the lens of "It is only a matter of time before the cyber attackers will get in. Here is what we are doing to detect signals so we can stop the hack before any damage is done and here is what we have found."

Organizations of course need to continue to prevent the hack, but the lens cannot be of one view only or be lopsided. Otherwise, there will be a big blind spot and a big surprise. The lens must equally be of both prevention and detection (with timely remediation).

While strategy, financials and operations are critical and must remain a priority, so must cybersecurity. Every organization must elevate cybersecurity so that it is also provided equal time and focus, because cybersecurity is critical. Every organization is at risk and must protect the **Crown Jewels**, because if the **Crown Jewels** are stolen, hijacked or damaged, it may be game over.

My research into the dozens and dozens of cases worldwide revealed that as cyber attackers broke in and hunted for the **Crown Jewels**, their behaviors and activities provided signals. In each case, however, these signals were either not monitored or missed by the organization or if someone did notice an anomaly, they either did not recognize it as a signal or it was never followed up.

Senior management and board oversight was missing or inadequate, so the cybersecurity was not up to par, and the attackers slipped through undetected and stole the data or inflicted other harm.

Regular dashboard reporting to the highest levels in the organization of the results generated from the system of Cyber Attack Signals and any risk mitigation action taken will ensure everyone remains knowledgeable, on the same page, and focused on staying one step ahead of the cyber attackers.

The dashboard report should show all of the Cyber Attack Signals for each **Crown Jewel** and in aggregate, and the status of risk mitigation of any anomalies detected.

With this dashboard reporting of the Cyber Attack Signals, senior management and the board of directors can ask key questions to make sure all **Crown Jewels** are monitored and early detection of cyber attackers and prompt risk mitigation is the focus, so that the hack is detected and stopped before any damage is done. The dashboard report should be provided not only to senior management, but also to either the entire board of directors or to a **cybersecurity committee** of the board.

Cyber risk is one of the most complex, dynamic and disruptive risks faced and it is time that every board consider formulating and implementing a dedicated board-level **cybersecurity committee.**

Most organizations currently have burdened the audit committee with oversight responsibilities over cybersecurity. However, the audit committee already has a full plate.

Beyond that, being able to effectively oversee cybersecurity requires specialized knowledge given the complexity of the topic, and the need to always look forward, given the dynamic nature of cyber risk with rapidly changing and evolving cyber threats.

It will be a challenge for audit committees to effectively oversee cybersecurity, because the audit committee is focused on audits, financial reporting and disclosures, and therefore, inherently the job is to look backward.

Asking the audit committee to do both jobs is asking too much.

Trying to stay on top of cyber risk and always looking forward, while also staying on top of financial risk and looking backward, is asking too much of the audit committee and is a recipe for oversight gaps, blind spots and ultimately, failure.

Just as there is at least one financial expert on the audit committee, there should be at least one cybersecurity expert on the cybersecurity committee, and the charter should outline the oversight responsibilities over cyber risk and the organization's cybersecurity program.

That way, the cybersecurity committee can focus on cyber risk and oversee cybersecurity adequately, with proper time devoted and with proper informational tools, such as the dashboard report of Cyber Attack Signals.

Formulating and implementing a cybersecurity committee at the board level is key to taking an organization's cybersecurity to the next level.

I predict organizations world-wide will heed my advice and implement a dedicated cybersecurity committee proactively at the board level. I also predict that eventually lawmakers and regulators will mandate it. Just as happened over time with the mandate for audit committee to oversee financial reporting risk.

In summary, using Cyber Attack Signals to detect cyber attackers early is the game changer for the entire organization, including at the highest levels.

Figure 5. Early detection of cyber attackers

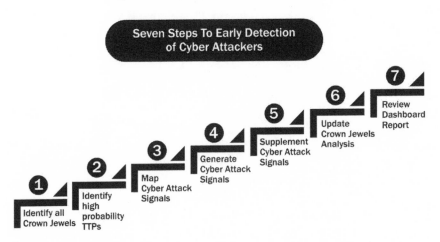

Figure 5 summarizes visually the seven steps necessary to properly implement *the game changer* and take cybersecurity to the next level.

Five key takeaways from this chapter

❑ Using Cyber Attack Signals to detect cyber attackers early is the game changer. To implement the game changer and take cybersecurity to the next level involves seven steps. Steps 1, 2 and 3 comprise performing **Crown Jewels** analysis.

○ All **Crown Jewels** must be identified. If any **Crown Jewels** are missed, it will be all downhill from this point on. The organization will always be one step behind the cyber attackers and will always have blind spots.

○ For each **Crown Jewel**, high-probability scenarios of TTPs must be identified that attackers could use to steal the **Crown Jewels** or inflict other harm.

○ Next, relevant Cyber Attack Signals to detect the attackers must be mapped in each step in the Cyber Attack Chain for each Crown Jewel. In that way, if for some reason a signal of the cyber attackers is missed in a particular step, another signal can detect the attackers in another step.

❏ Step 4 is to identify all data sources and leverage the SIEM or another tool to generate the Cyber Attack Signals. The key to success is to make sure the Cyber Attack Signals are mapped to the **Crown Jewels** to focus on detecting cyber attackers' behavior early in the Cyber Attack Chain, regardless of whether the **Crown Jewels** are on the premises or in the cloud.

❏ Step 5 is to implement honeypots, threat hunting and threat scouts to supplement the system of Cyber Attack Signals so as to increase the chances of detecting the cyber attackers in time.

❏ Step 6 is to update the **Crown Jewels** analysis periodically so as to incorporate significant changes, threats or risk factors. **Crown Jewels** analysis is the beginning and not the end of the game-winning strategy, and is a dynamic and not a one-time exercise in order to stay one step ahead of the cyber attackers. As such, the analysis will need to be updated periodically to reflect new, high-probability threats or to reflect significant changes that occur in the organization impacting the **Crown Jewels**.

❏ Step 7 is to report Cyber Attack Signals in a dashboard to the highest levels (i.e. senior management and board of directors) regularly and promptly. This reporting will facilitate proper and timely oversight from the highest levels. Cybersecurity cannot be a back-office IT issue; instead it must be front and center and a boardroom issue and a priority. Cyber risk is one of the most significant and disruptive risks faced by almost every organization and protecting the **Crown Jewels** must be a top priority at the highest levels.

Every organization should implement a dedicated cybersecurity committee at the board level to optimally oversee cyber risk and the cybersecurity program. This best practice will take the organization's cybersecurity to the next level.

Chapter 13

The Closing

Chapter 13

The Closing

The early-detection method in this book is about identifying the ways cyber attackers could get to the **Crown Jewels**, and then mapping the **Crown Jewels** to relevant Cyber Attack Signals focused on cyber attackers' behavior to detect the attackers early in the Cyber Attack Chain.

It is only a matter of time before the cyber attackers will break in. Detecting the attackers early and shutting the attackers down is the key to preventing a cyber disaster. The method and the system of Cyber Attack Signals covered in this book is the game changer.

As we wrap up, however, we need to look ahead and recognize that the cyber attackers are always looking for new ways to get to the **Crown Jewels** and they have identified 1) suppliers, such as technology providers, and 2) IoT devices, as two weak links in the chain and a backdoor to get to the **Crown Jewels** under the radar.

Just look at the more recent SolarWinds hack. It is one of the largest hacks and supply chain compromises in history. SolarWinds is a cybersecurity software provider to over 300,000 organizations worldwide. The attackers penetrated thousands of organizations by simply penetrating SolarWinds.

They broke into the company's software update process undetected and inserted malware into one of its products. As thousands of customers downloaded the software update, they also downloaded the malware. 18,000 organizations worldwide unknowingly downloaded the backdoor. While the attackers did not activate the backdoor for all, they did activate the malware in hundreds of organizations across North America, Europe, Middle East and Asia.

The malware allowed the attackers to move laterally, steal privileged users' credentials, read emails and access **Crown Jewels**, communicate with its command and control servers and exfiltrate sensitive data.

The hack went undetected for over nine months, until FireEye, a cyber-security provider and a customer of SolarWinds first discovered and disclosed the hack.[1]

While the attackers were sophisticated, certain Cyber Attack Signals, as previously covered in this book, were missed and could have been detected in time to stop the hack. These signals were in the lateral movement and command and control steps in the Cyber Attack Chain:

❑ **abnormal logons**
The attackers used multiple IP addresses to remotely login using stolen privileged users' accounts and credentials. However, the IP addresses used were "impossible travel" (i.e. a person could not realistically travel between geographic locations of the IP addresses during the time period of the logins.) Analyzing the time and geographic location of the IP addresses and also comparing to a baseline of normal login would have detected this Cyber Attack Signal.

❑ **privileged users' behavior**
The attackers stole privileged users' credentials and used it to access the server that stored Security Assertion Markup Language (SAML) certificates. With this access, they were able to forge SAML tokens and sign it with the stolen certificates. This allowed the attackers access to services that trust SAML tokens, such as hosted email services, hosted business intelligence applications, and file storage services (such as SharePoint). Monitoring the **Crown Jewel** (i.e. server that stored SAML certificates) for users access, type of users accessing it, when, how often and what tasks were being performed, and looking for any anomalous activity, would have detected this Cyber Attack Signal.

❑ **SMB anomalies**
The attackers exploited SMB in Microsoft Windows to insert tools for remote access and to propagate malware and perform lateral movement. They routinely removed their tools once remote access was achieved. Analyzing SMB sessions for anomalous activity such

as a delete-create-execute-delete-create pattern in a short amount of time or tasks being modified or executing new or unknown binaries would have detected this Cyber Attack Signal.

❑ **C&C communications**

The backdoor in the SolarWinds software update file, with the name SolarWinds.Orion.Core.BusinessLayer.dll, would lay dormant for up to two weeks, then it would attempt to communicate with a C&C server with a domain name of avsvmcloud.com. Monitoring for anomalous communications such as attempts to communicate with an unusual domain within a short amount of time from a key event such as a software update would have detected this Cyber Attack Signal.

So, we need to anticipate that cyber attackers will increasingly hunt for and compromise a supplier first, such as a technology provider, in order to penetrate the target organization. One must recognize this potential backdoor and monitor closely for Cyber Attack Signals, in particular at the time of software updates, so one can detect the attacker in time.

We also need to anticipate that cyber attackers will increasingly hunt for IoT devices to compromise, and then pivot and hunt for the **Crown Jewels.**

Why? Because 1) there is widespread adoption of IoT devices worldwide, 2) the devices can be easily discovered by searching the Internet and easily hacked because of weak security from the manufacturer, 3) consumers and organizations are not following security best practices when installing or activating the devices, 4) the devices are not being patched (a lot of times there is no way to patch), and 5) the devices frequently are not thought of as capable of providing a path to the **Crown Jewels** and are ignored and not monitored to detect anomalies.

Consider the following case involving IoT. While it occurred a few years ago, it has enormous relevance as we look ahead.

The U.S. Federal Trade Commission (FTC) sued ASUSTeK Computer, Inc. (ASUS), a Taiwan-based company, charging that ASUS had sold its routers and cloud services with critical security flaws.[2]

Cyber attackers had scanned the Internet and located vulnerable ASUS routers and exploited the security flaws to gain unauthorized access. ASUS had sold more than 918,000 routers in the U.S.

The flaws allowed anyone to change security settings easily via a web-based control panel remotely. Other flaws, included a default generic login credential on every router — username "admin" and password "admin" — which could easily be guessed by anyone. ASUS settled the charges and agreed to establish and maintain a comprehensive security program that will be subject to independent audits for 20 years.

The ASUS case was a warning shot of how vulnerable IoT devices are. Unfortunately, the warning has not yet been taken seriously. For example, a simple search on the Internet using one of the IoT search engines will reveal thousands of IoT devices, such as routers with unchanged manufacturer default usernames and passwords, and details of each of the devices, such as the IP address, organization name and country of location, etc.

Imagine this type of information in the hands of the attackers. You get the picture of what can happen next.

A similar major risk is an attack on any other type of vulnerable IoT device (e.g. webcam, sensor, smart printer, etc.) to make the intrusion, and then pivoting to get to the **Crown Jewels**.

As IoT devices are increasingly adopted by individuals and organizations worldwide, cyber attackers will also increasingly hunt for these devices. So the devices must be a focus and the early-detection method in this book ensures that IoT devices are inventoried and analyzed as part of the **Crown Jewels** analysis as a potential pathway to the **Crown Jewels**, and then mapped to Cyber Attack Signals to detect the cyber attackers early.

Also, two critical steps you can take at home are: (a) segment your home network by separating your IoT devices (e.g. smart TV, webcam, etc.) into one router and your devices with data (e.g. smart phone, laptop or desktop) into another router, or use the micro segment feature in your router to segment, so that a cyber attacker cannot easily pivot from an IoT device to a device with data and steal it or pivot from that device to break into your work network; and (b) change the factory default passwords in your IoT devices to strong, complex passwords, so a cyber attacker cannot easily crack it and break into your home network.

Appendix A is a self-assessment checklist so you can quickly evaluate your organization's cybersecurity.

I hope you enjoyed the book. Be sure to implement the best practices and the game-changing, early-detection method covered in this book right away, to take your cybersecurity to the next level, and to stay one step ahead of the cyber attackers.

Also, please go to my website at www.saihuda.com for additional resources so you can stay proactive.

I wish you much success.

Endnotes

Chapter 1: The Opening

1 "How Facebook Hackers Compromised 30 Million Accounts", *Wired*, October 12, 2018 https://www.wired.com/story/how-facebook-hackers-compromised-30-million-accounts/

2 "SingHealth's IT System Target of Cyber attack", SingHealth Press Release, July 20, 2018 https://www.singhealth.com.sg/AboutSingHealth/CorporateOverview/Newsroom/NewsReleases/2018/Pages/cyber attack.aspx

3 "British Airways customer data theft between August 21, 2018 and September 5, 2018", British Airways https://www.britishairways.com/en-gb/information/incident/data-theft/latest-information

4 "Forecast: Internet of Things (IoT) – Endpoints and Associated Services, Worldwide", Gartner, December 21, 2017 https://www.gartner.com/doc/3840665/forecast-Internet-things--endpoints

5 "How Many Internet Users Will the World Have in 2022, and in 2030?", Cybersecurity Ventures, July 19, 2018 https://cybersecurityventures.com/how-many-Internet-users-will-the-world-have-in-2022-and-in-2030/

Chapter 2: The Cyber Attack Chain and Signals

1 U.S. Department of Homeland Security (DHS) and Federal Bureau of Investigation (FBI) joint Technical Alert TA18-074A "Russian Government Cyber Activity Targeting Energy and Other Critical Infrastructure Sectors" dated March 15, 2018 https://www.us-cert.gov/ncas/alerts/TA18-074A

2 Lockheed Martin's Intrusion Kill Chain as introduced in 2011 in "Intelligence-Driven Computer Network Defense Informed by Analysis of Adversary Campaigns and Intrusion Kill Chains" https://www.lockheedmartin.com/content/dam/lockheed-martin/rms/documents/cyber/LM-White-Paper-Intel-Driven-Defense.pdf

3 MITRE's Cyber Attack Lifecycle or Adversarial Tactics, Techniques and Common Knowledge (ATT&CK) for Enterprise https://attack.mitre.org/wiki/Introduction_and_Overview

4 Mandiant, a FireEye Company's Attack LifeCycle https://www.fireeye.com/content/dam/fireeye-www/services/pdfs/ds-threatspace.pdf

Chapter 3: Early Detection is the Game Changer

1 2018 Study on Global Megatrends in Cybersecurity, Benchmark research sponsored by Raytheon, independently conducted by Ponemon Institute, February 2018

2 MITRE's Cyber Analytic Repository (CAR), a knowledgebase of analytics based on MITRE's Adversary Tactics, Techniques and Common Knowledge (ATT&CK) adversary model https://car.mitre.org/wiki/Main_Page

3 *Finding Cyber Threat with ATT&CK-Based Analytics*, MITRE Technical Report, June 2017 https://www.mitre.org/sites/default/files/publications/16-3713-finding-cyber-threats%20with%20att%26ck-based-analytics.pdf

4 "OWASP Top 10: The Ten Most Critical Web Application Security Risks", published by Open Web Application Security Project (OWASP) https://www.owasp.org/index.php/Category:OWASP_Top_Ten_Project

5 "OWASP Top IoT Vulnerabilities", published by Open Web Application Security Project (OWASP) https://www.owasp.org/index.php/OWASP_Internet_of_Things_Project#tab=IoT_Vulnerabilities

Chapter 4: Missed Signals in 3 Billion User Accounts Theft

1 "Verizon announces it has completed acquisition of Yahoo under new subsidiary named Oath", June 13, 2017 https://www.verizon.com/about/news/verizon-completes-yahoo-acquisition-creating-diverse-house-50-brands-under-new-oath-subsidiary

2 "Verizon announces it will acquire Yahoo for $4.83 billion", July 25, 2016 https://www.verizon.com/about/news/verizon-acquire-yahoos-operating-business

3 "Verizon announces Yahoo has agreed to reduce the price Verizon will pay to acquire Yahoo by $350 million", February 21, 2017 https://www.verizon.com/about/news/verizon-and-yahoo-amend-terms-definitive-agreement

4 "Yahoo, now part of Oath, notice to additional users affected by August 2013 data breach, disclosing that all 3 billion Yahoo user account data was stolen", October 3, 2017 https://www.oath.com/press/yahoo-provides-notice-to-additional-users-affected-by-previously/

5 James Rogers, "Yahoo hack: the Exxon Valdez of security breaches", Fox News, December 15, 2016 http://www.foxnews.com/tech/2016/12/15/yahoo-hack-exxon-valdez-security-breaches.html

6 "U.S. Charges Russian FSB Officers and their Criminal Conspirators for Hacking Yahoo and Millions of Email Account", March 15, 2017 https://www.justice.gov/opa/pr/us-charges-russian-fsb-officers-and-their-criminal-conspirators-hacking-yahoo-and-millions

7 "An Important Message to Users on Security", Yahoo, September 22, 2016 https://www.businesswire.com/news/home/20160922006198/en/

8 "Yahoo says about 32 million accounts accessed using 'forged cookies' ", March 1, 2017 https://www.businessinsider.com/r-yahoo-says-about-32-mln-accounts-accessed-using-forged-cookies-2017-3

9 U.S. Securities and Exchange Commission (SEC) Press Release announcing $35 million penalty to settle charges against entity formerly known as Yahoo! Inc., April 24, 2018 https://www.sec.gov/news/press-release/2018-71

Chapter 5: Equifax: Patch Window

1 The Common Vulnerability and Exposures (CVEs) https://www.cvedetails.com

2 The U.S. National Vulnerability Database https://nvd.nist.gov

3 Equifax first disclosed the data breach impacting 143 million consumers on September 7, 2017 publicly through a press release. https://investor.equifax.com/news-and-events/news/2017/09-07-2017-213000628

4 Equifax disclosed on October 2, 2017 that another 2.5 million consumers were impacted. https://investor.equifax.com/news-and-events/news/2017/10-02-2017-213238821

5 Equifax disclosed on March 1, 2018 that additional 2.4 million consumers were impacted with their name and partial driver's license information stolen by cyber attackers. https://investor.equifax.com/news-and-events/news/2018/03-01-2018-140531340

6 Apache Software Foundation Media Alert, stating that Apache Struts vulnerability announced on March 7, 2017 via Security Bulletin S2-045 and patch issued same day and CVE-2017-5638 reported same day https://blogs.apache.org/foundation/entry/media-alert-the-apache-software

7 The cybersecurity firm Mandiant hired by Equifax to conduct forensic review of the data breach reported that cyber attackers were roaming undetected inside Equifax's computer network since March 10, 2017. https://nypost.com/2017/09/20/cyber attackers-have-been-hiding-in-equifaxs-computer-network-for-months/?utm_campaign=iosapp&utm_source=mail_app

8 The Equifax Data Breach, Majority Staff Report, Committee on Oversight and Government Reform, U.S. House of Representatives, December 2018

9 The Equifax Data Breach, Majority Staff Report, U.S. House of Representatives

10 Equifax disclosed on September 15, 2017 further details and that it discovered the data breach on July 29, 2017 and upon realizing it was from the Apache Struts vulnerability

it implemented the patch on July 30, 2017. https://investor.equifax.com/news-and-events/news/2017/09-15-2017-224018832

11 Testimony of Richard F. Smith, former CEO, Equifax, before U.S. House Committee on Energy and Commerce, October 3, 2017 https://docs.house.gov/meetings/IF/IF17/20171003/106455/HHRG-115-IF17-Wstate-SmithR-20171003.pdf

12 Testimony of Richard F. Smith before U.S. House Committee, October 3, 2017

Chapter 6: Anthem: Abnormal Logons

1 *Report of the Multistate Targeted Market Conduct and Financial Examination of Anthem Insurance Companies, Inc. and its Affiliates*, December 1, 2016 http://www.insurance.ca.gov/0400-news/0100-press-releases/2016/upload/Anthem-Examination-Report-AM-2016-12-01.pdf

2 Statement regarding cyber attack against Anthem, Anthem press release, February 5, 2015 https://www.anthem.com/press/wisconsin/statement-regarding-cyber-attack-against-anthem/

3 Anthem Multistate Regulatory Settlement Agreement, December 1, 2016 http://www.insurance.ca.gov/0400-news/0100-press-releases/2016/upload/Fully-Executed-RSA-2.PDF

4 Anthem Data Breach Class Action Settlement, February 1, 2018 http://www.databreach-settlement.com/

Chapter 7: U.S. OPM: Privileged Users' Behavior

1 OPM Cybersecurity Incidents https://www.opm.gov/cybersecurity/cybersecurity-incidents/#WhatHappened

2 OPM Cybersecurity Incidents FAQs https://www.opm.gov/cybersecurity/faqs/

3 *The OPM Data Breach*, Committee on Oversight and Government Reform, U.S. House of Representatives, Minority Staff Report, September 2016 https://oversight.house.gov/wp-content/uploads/2016/09/The-OPM-Data-Breach-How-the-Government-Jeopardized-Our-National-Security-for-More-than-a-Generation.pdf

4 *The OPM Data Breach*, Committee on Oversight and Government Reform, U.S. House of Representatives, Democratic Memorandum, September 2016 https://democrats-oversight.house.gov/sites/democrats.oversight.house.gov/files/documents/2016-09-06.Democratic%20Memo%20on%20OPM%20Data%20Breach%20Investigation.pdf

5 *The OPM Data Breach Hearing Transcript*, Committee on Oversight and Government Reform, U.S House of Representatives, June 24, 2015 https://oversight.house.gov/wp-

content/uploads/2015/06/2015-06-24-FC-OPM-DATA-BREACH-PART-II.GO175001.
pdf

6 *The OPM Data Breach*, Committee on Oversight and Government Reform, U.S. House
of Representatives, Democratic Memorandum, September 2016

7 *The OPM Data Breach Hearing Transcript*, Committee on Oversight and Government
Reform, U.S House of Representatives, June 24, 2015

8 Monitoring Active Directory for Signs of Compromise, Microsoft, May 31, 2017 https://
docs.microsoft.com/en-us/windows-server/identity/ad-ds/plan/security-best-practices/
monitoring-active-directory-for-signs-of-compromise

9 Appendix L: Events to Monitor, Microsoft, May 31, 2017 https://docs.microsoft.com/
en-us/windows-server/identity/ad-ds/plan/appendix-l--events-to-monitor

Chapter 8: NHS England: Ransomware Signals

1 U.S. Department of Justice (DOJ) Indictment, U.S. District Court, District of New
Jersey, November 26, 2018 https://www.justice.gov/opa/press-release/file/1114741/
download

2 "Confidential Report: Atlanta's cyber attack could cost taxpayers $17 million",
Stephen Deere, Atlanta Journal-Constitution, August 1, 2018 https://www.
ajc.com/news/confidential-report-atlanta-cyber-attack-could-hit-million/
GAljmndAF3EQdVWlMcXS0K/?icmp=np_inform_variation-control

3 Andy Greenberg, "The Untold Story of NotPetya, the Most Devastating Cyber attack in
History", *Wired*, August 8, 2018 https://www.wired.com/story/notpetya-cyber attack-
ukraine-russia-code-crashed-the-world/

4 United States Computer Emergency Readiness Team (US-CERT) Alert TA17-181A,
NotPetya Ransomware https://www.us-cert.gov/ncas/alerts/TA17-181A

5 Merck & Co., Inc. U.S. SEC Form 10-K Annual Report, February 27, 2018 http://www.
annualreports.com/HostedData/AnnualReports/PDF/NYSE_MRK_2017.pdf

6 Microsoft Security Bulletin MS17-010-Critical, March 14, 2017 https://docs.microsoft.
com/en-us/security-updates/SecurityBulletins/2017/ms17-010

7 The Common Vulnerability and Exposures (CVEs) https://www.cvedetails.com/
vulnerability-list/year-2017/month-3/March.html

8 United States Computer Emergency Readiness Team (US-CERT) Alert TA17-132A,
Indicators Associated With WannaCry Ransomware, May 12, 2017 https://www.us-cert.
gov/ncas/alerts/TA17-132A

9 "Investigation: WannaCry cyber attack and the NHS", U.K. Department of Health Report by Comptroller and Auditor General, National Audit Office, October 24, 2017 https://www.nao.org.uk/wp-content/uploads/2017/10/Investigation-WannaCry-cyber-attack-and-the-NHS.pdf

Chapter 9: U.S. DNC: Unusual Logs Behavior

1 U.S. Department of Justice (DOJ) Indictment, U.S. District Court, District of Columbia, July 13, 2018 https://www.justice.gov/file/1080281/download

2 U.S. Intelligence Community Assessment, Declassified Report, Assessing Russian Activities and Intentions in Recent US Elections, Office of Director of National Intelligence, January 6, 2017

3 Matthew Chance, "Julian Assange: a 'lot more material coming' on U.S. elections", CNN, July 27, 2016 https://edition.cnn.com/2016/07/26/politics/julian-assange-dnc-email-leak-hack/

4 *Detecting Lateral movement through Tracking Event Logs*, Japan Computer Emergency Response Team Coordination Center (JPCERTCC), June 2017 https://www.jpcert.or.jp/english/pub/sr/20170612ac-ir_research_en.pdf

Chapter 10: Target: ICMP Packets

1 *A "Kill Chain" Analysis of the 2013 Target Data Breach*, Majority Staff Report, Committee on Commerce, Science, and Transportation, U.S. Senate, March 26, 2014

2 *A "Kill Chain" Analysis*, Majority Staff Report, U.S. Senate

3 *A "Kill Chain" Analysis*, Majority Staff Report, U.S. Senate

4 Testimony of John Mulligan, Target Executive Vice President and Chief Financial Officer, before the U.S. Senate Committee on the Judiciary, February 2, 2014

5 "Target Confirms Unauthorized Access to Payment Card Data in U.S. Stores", December 19, 2013 http://pressroom.target.com/news/target-confirms-unauthorized-access-to-payment-card-data-in-u-s-stores

6 "Target provides update on data breach and financial performance", January 10, 2014 https://corporate.target.com/press/releases/2014/01/target-provides-update-on-data-breach-and-financial

Chapter 11: SingHealth: C&C Communications

1 "Singapore Tops Intel and Juniper Ranking of Top 20 Global Smart Cities", *The Straits Times*, March 14, 2018 https://www.straitstimes.com/business/spore-pips-london-ny-to-top-global-smart-city-ranking

2 "SingHealth's IT System Target of Cyber attack", SingHealth Press Release, July 20, 2018 https://www.singhealth.com.sg/AboutSingHealth/CorporateOverview/Newsroom/NewsReleases/2018/Pages/cyber attack.aspx

3 Statement by Singapore Minister-in-Charge of Cybersecurity, on cyber attack on SingHealth's IT system, during Parliamentary Sitting, August 6, 2018 https://www.mci.gov.sg/pressroom/news-and-stories/pressroom/2018/8/statement-by-mr-s-iswaran-on--cyber-attack-on-singhealth-it-system-during-parl-sitting-on-6-aug-2018?page=5

4 "SingHealth Committee of Inquiry (COI): Hackers tried to attack network again on July 19 amid probe", *The Straits Times*, October 5, 2018 https://www.straitstimes.com/singapore/coi-on-singhealth-data-breach-hackers-tried-to-attack-network-again-on-july-19-amid

5 "Committee of Inquiry (COI) on SingHealth cyber attack: Server accessed by hackers missed security updates for over a year", *The Straits Times*, September 28, 2018 https://www.straitstimes.com/singapore/server-accessed-by-hackers-missed-security-updates-for-over-a-year

6 "Committee of Inquiry (COI) on SingHealth cyber attack: Failings in judgment, organization exposed", *The Straits Times*, September 26, 2018 https://www.straitstimes.com/singapore/failings-in-judgement-organisation-exposed-as-cyber-attack-coi-grills-singhealth-risk-man

Chapter 12: Seven Steps to Detect Cyber Attackers Early

1 Chris Morris, "465,000 Pacemakers Recalled on Hacking Fears", *Fortune*, August 31, 2017 http://fortune.com/2017/08/31/pacemaker-recall-fda/

2 Richard Chirgwin, "Finns Chilling as DDoS Knocks Out Building Control System", *The Register*, November 9, 2016 https://www.theregister.co.uk/2016/11/09/finns_chilling_as_ddos_knocks_out_building_control_system/

3 Alfred Ng, "Hackers Should Be Pumped about Gas Station Security Flaws", CNET, March 12, 2018 https://www.cnet.com/news/gas-stations-online-are-easy-access-for-managers-and-hackers/

4 *The Dangers of Smart City Hacking*, IBM X-Force Red and Threatcare Ethical Hacking Whitepaper, IBM, August 2018 https://www-01.ibm.com/common/ssi/cgi-bin/ssialias?htmlfid=75018475USEN

5 Internet of Threats, Benchmarking Survey, IBM Institute for Business Value (IBV), March 2018

6 MITRE's Adversarial Tactics, Techniques and Common Knowledge (ATT&CK) for Enterprise https://attack.mitre.org/wiki/Technique_Matrix

7 "OWASP Top: The Ten Most Critical Web Application Security Risks", published by Open Web Application Security Project (OWASP) https://www.owasp.org/index.php/Category:OWASP_Top_Ten_Project

8 "OWASP Top IoT Vulnerabilities", published by Open Web Application Security Project (OWASP) https://www.owasp.org/index.php/OWASP_Internet_of_Things_Project#tab=IoT_Vulnerabilities

9 MITRE's Cyber Analytic Repository (CAR), a knowledgebase of analytics based on MITRE's Adversary Tactics, Techniques and Common Knowledge (ATT&CK) adversary model https://car.mitre.org/wiki/Main_Page

10 *Finding Cyber Threat with ATT&CK-Based Analytics, MITRE Technical Report*, June 2017 https://www.mitre.org/sites/default/files/publications/16-3713-finding-cyber-threats%20with%20att%26ck-based-analytics.pdf

11 Eric Newcomer, "Uber Paid Hackers to Delete Stolen Data on 57 Million People", Bloomberg, November 21, 2017 https://www.bloomberg.com/news/articles/2017-11-21/uber-concealed-cyber attack-that-exposed-57-million-people-s-data

12 "Money Doesn't Grow on Trees, but it's Growing in the Cloud", RedLock CSI Team, RedLock, October 5, 2017 https://redlock.io/blog/kubernetes-cloud-security-breach-bitcoin-mining

Chapter 13: The Closing

1 "Highly Evasive Attacker Leverages SolarWinds Supply Chain to Compromise Multiple Global Victims With SUNBURST Backdoor", FireEye, December 13, 2020 https://www.fireeye.com/blog/threat-research/2020/12/evasive-attacker-leverages-solarwinds-supply-chain-compromises-with-sunburst-backdoor.html

2 "ASUS Settles FTC Charges that Insecure Home Routers and 'Cloud' Services Put Consumers' Privacy at Risk", FTC Press Release, February 23, 2016 https://www.ftc.gov/news-events/press-releases/2016/02/asus-settles-ftc-charges-insecure-home-routers-cloud-services-put

APPENDIX A

SELF-ASSESSMENT CHECKLIST: ARE YOU AT RISK?

Answer the following questions to assess your organization's ability to detect cyber attackers early. You in each question refers to you and/or a supplier acting for you — you may have out-sourced your cybersecurity or cyber infrastructure to them (e.g. a cloud technology provider).

1. Have you defined adequately what should be your **Crown Jewels**?   Yes   No

2. Have you completed an inventory to capture **all** of your **Crown Jewels**?   Yes   No

3. Have you identified the ways cyber attackers could very likely get to   Yes   No
   the **Crown Jewels** including using IoT and steal or hijack and disrupt
   operations?

4. Have you developed a set of signals focused on cyber attackers   Yes   No
   behavior to monitor, mapped to the **Crown Jewels** that would
   detect the attackers?

5. Do you have an automated system implemented to monitor **all** of   Yes   No
   your **Crown Jewels** to detect cyber attackers trying to steal or
   hijack the **Crown Jewels**?

6. Do you update the ways cyber attackers could very likely get to   Yes   No
   the **Crown Jewels** or the signals of cyber attackers behavior
   to monitor, if any new events happen that could impact the **Crown
   Jewels** or if new threats emerge?

7. Do you have a dashboard of automated monitoring results and   Yes   No
   signals of potential cyber attackers activity that you report regularly to
   the highest levels (i.e. senior management and board of directors)?

8. Do you have a dedicated team proactively hunting for signals of   Yes   No
   cyber attackers, instead of reacting to alerts?

9. Do you use gaming or simulations to provide real-world training to   Yes   No
   your entire organization to detect potential cyber attackers activity?

10. Do you use honeypots to detect cyber attackers?   Yes   No

Here is the self-assessment scoring scale. Each "Yes" answer is worth 10 points.

Ability to Detect Cyber attackers Early	Points
Strong	90 - 100
Needs Some Improvement	70 - 80
Weak	less than 70

If you scored less than 70 points, you are at a weak level. That means you are very unlikely to detect the cyber attackers in time and are at high risk of the cyber attackers evading your defense and stealing or hijacking your **Crown Jewels**.

185

APPENDIX B

TOP 15 CYBER ATTACK SIGNALS

CYBER ATTACK CHAIN STEP	CYBER ATTACK SIGNALS	SUMMARY
Intrusion	Patch Window	Time period between a known vulnerability and the fix or interim workaround, highlights the window that cyber attackers have to break in. The longer the patch window, the greater the exposure for an intrusion. Also, the vulnerability type provides insight into attackers probable exploit method, attack timeline and expected behavior.
	Web Shell	Anomalous activity, such as unusual length of time period of logon to webserver or JPG file making requests with POST parameters, indicating cyber attackers installing a web shell or have installed a web shell, such as through SQL injection, cross-site scripting or file processing vulnerabilities, to make the intrusion.
Lateral Movement	Abnormal Logons	Anomalies in logons, compared to normal logon pattern thresholds in terms of user type, role, level, time, frequency, tasks, source and destination, including devices such as IoT, indicating signals of cyber attackers trying to steal credentials or using stolen credentials or using brute force.
	Privileged Users' Behavior	Anomalous activity, compared to normal behavior pattern thresholds, of privileged users such as Admin users and others, in terms of user types, permissions, logon times, frequency, duration, tasks, source and destination, based on privilege level, role and job duties.
	WMI Anomalies	Abnormal activity with Windows Management Instrumentation (WMI), which is installed in all Windows systems for use by administrators. Event tracking can trigger alerts such as _InstanceCreationEvent, _InstanceDeletionEvent or _ClassCreation Event, if unusual for a user or user type using WMI remotely or locally.
	Internal Reconnaissance Signals	Anomalous scripts running on email, web or file servers or domain controllers, or output from scripts, such as queries listing all valid SPNs (Service Principal Names) in the domain controller with details such as the service name, port number and the server it is running on, or Windows scheduled tasks running commands to collect screen shots or other information in the Temp folder such as the command "C:\Windows\Temp\scr.exe" are signals that it is most probably cyber attackers performing internal reconnaissance and moving laterally.
	Malware Signals	Anomalous activities that signal attempted malware propagation for different time windows (i.e. hourly, daily, etc.), systems, files, devices including IoT and network services, such as many computers pinging the same host over 24 to 48 hours (indicating phishing and most probably unsuspecting users downloading malware from malicious web site) or process modifies a file in systems directory or document files or IoT devices attempting communications with an IP address.

	Ransomware Signals	Anomalous activities indicating early signs of ransomware being installed or propagated or activated, such as creation of several new files .pky (public encryption key), .res (command and control communications), .eky (private encryption key) or deletion of backup files (e.g. in shared network drive).
	Malicious PowerShell	Anomalies in commands and scripts executed, outputs and transcripts of activity signal that it is most probably cyber attackers moving laterally and exploiting PowerShell, scripting language for administrators. PowerShell 5.0 provides three types of logging: module, script block and transcription. Logging should be enabled for signals such as abnormal users running the scripts, unusual start and end times, suspicious buzzwords or obfuscation characters in the scripts such as + ' $ % or other odd characters to evade detection.
	RDP Signals	Remote Desktop Protocol (RDP) enables a user such as a system administrator or help desk staff to use a graphical interface to connect to another computer in a network. Cyber attackers frequently use RDP. Key is to inventory users with authorized RDP access, then determine normal behavior patterns in terms of the RDP users, time windows, processes and tasks, sources and destinations and detect anomalies such as abnormal RDP users or RDP source or destination logons, a single user with RDP logons from multiple source systems, RDP logons at unusual times for authorized RDP user, .reg file that alters the Windows registry or patch file that alters termsvrl.dll to allow RDP.
	SMB Anomalies	Server Message Block (SMB) is a protocol in Microsoft Windows that enables remotely managing files, file sharing, printing and directory share among other functions in a network. Use of PsExec and C$, ADMIN$, or IPC$ shares are red flags. Cyber attackers frequently use these shares to exploit SMB and these are signals of the attacker at work, propagating malware or moving laterally.
	Unusual Logs Behavior	Any event logs removed, stopped or cleared with details such as user details, date, time, type of log, command executed to impact the event log, asset impacted, source, destination, etc. will provide a signal that it is most probably cyber attackers moving laterally and hiding their tracks.
Command and Control (C&C)	C&C Communications	Anomalous activities could be signals of attempted malware, ransomware or cryptomining communications with a C&C server, so the network traffic baseline should be determined (i.e. normal communication patterns, data volume, etc.) for different time windows (i.e. hourly, daily, etc.), users, devices including IoT and services, including API communications, in order to identify the anomalies. Once the normal patterns are determined, monitoring can be activated to detect common signals as well as any anomalies to normal patterns.
	ICMP Packets	ICMP is Internet Control Message Protocol, a widely used method that uses packets containing messages, typically error or query messages, to enable servers and routers inside a network to communicate. The size or the frequency and source and destination of the ICMP packets going back and forth between servers and routers is a signal of data exfiltration and a data theft about to happen. If the size of the ICMP packet is above normal, it most probably indicates it contains stolen data. Or if the frequency or source and destination are abnormal, it could be a signal of the data being moved internally prior to the exfiltration.
	Hidden Tunnels	Cyber attackers frequently will use HTTP, HTTPS or DNS tunnels to establish communications between a compromised computer, server, database or IoT device inside the network with their Command and Control (C&C) server to propagate malware or ransomware or do a dry run of data exfiltration before proceeding with full exfiltration. A key step is to establish HTTP, HTTPS or DNS traffic baseline thresholds, based on history, for timely detection, tracking, reporting and resolution of anomalies.

About the Author

Sai Huda is a globally recognized risk and cybersecurity expert, technology visionary and business leader, with more than 20 years of hands-on experience.

He served seven years as General Manager, Risk, Information Security and Compliance Solutions at Fidelity National Information Services, Inc. (FIS), a Fortune 500 company serving more than 20,000 clients globally. Under his leadership, FIS attained number 1 ranking in Chartis RiskTech100®.

Prior to FIS, he was the founder and CEO of Compliance Coach, Inc., an innovative company providing risk management software and consulting services to more than 1,500 clients in financial services, healthcare and government sectors. Compliance Coach helped clients manage Information Security, Operational and Compliance risks. Compliance Coach was acquired by FIS.

He serves as an expert consultant and advises board and senior management on risk and cybersecurity best practices. He is also a frequent keynote speaker at industry conferences. To find out more, visit the author's website at www.saihuda.com.

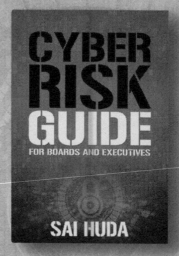

Made in the USA
Las Vegas, NV
12 August 2021

28012678R00116